# PRIESTS

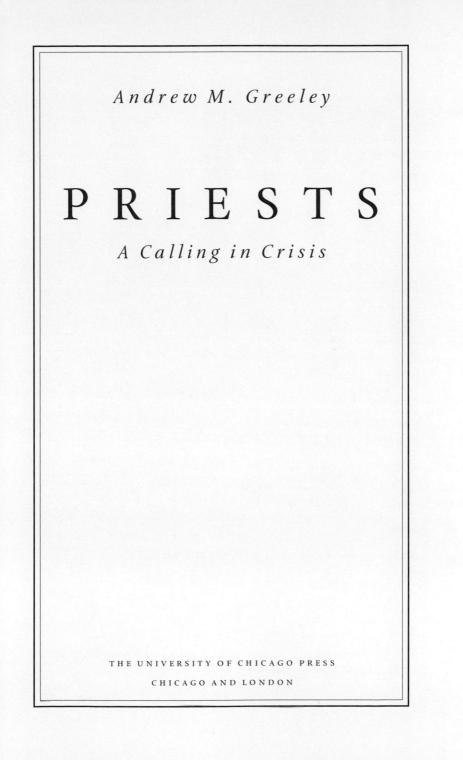

*Andrew M. Greeley*

# PRIESTS

*A Calling in Crisis*

THE UNIVERSITY OF CHICAGO PRESS

CHICAGO AND LONDON

Andrew M. Greeley is a prolific author who is also on the staff of the National Opinion Research Center at the University of Chicago and professor of social science at the University of Arizona. His nonfiction books include *Confessions of a Parish Priest, Religious Change in America, The Catholic Imagination,* and *The Catholic Revolution.*

The University of Chicago Press, Chicago 60637
The University of Chicago Press, Ltd., London
© 2004 by The University of Chicago
All rights reserved. Published 2004
Printed in the United States of America

13 12 11 10 09 08 07 06 05 04     2 3 4 5

ISBN: 0-226-30644-5 (cloth)

Library of Congress Cataloging-in-Publication Data

Greeley, Andrew M., 1928–
    Priests : a calling in crisis / Andrew M. Greeley.
        p. cm.
    Includes bibliographical references (p. ) and index.
    ISBN 0-226-30644-5 (cloth : alk. paper)
    1. Catholic Church—Clergy—Sexual behavior. 2. Catholic Church—Clergy. 3. Child sexual abuse—Religious aspects—Catholic Church. 4. Child sexual abuse by clergy. 5. Vatican Council (2nd : 1962–1965) I. Title.

BX1912.G34 2004
262′.142—dc22

2003059698

*To the honored memory of John Brennan,*
*a brave man who launched the first* Los Angeles Times
*study and thus provided the Catholic Church in the United States*
*with research that would have cost hundreds of thousands*
*of dollars, research that it did not want*
*and still doesn't.*

# CONTENTS

# ACKNOWLEDGMENTS

I am grateful for the encouraging comments of Father Leo Mahon, Monsignor Tomas O'Cahalaine, Michael Hout, Mark Chaves, Father Bradley Schaefer S.J., Dr. Paul McHugh, Tom Smith, and Father David Tracy.

I am also grateful for the help of the *Los Angeles Times* survey unit, especially Susan Pinkus and Sarah Vaughn, and Larry Stammer, the religion writer of the *Times,* and the advice of Paula Barker Duffy and John Tryneski of the University of Chicago Press.

*I don't think it's any worse than the
Protestant Reformation.*
AUXILIARY BISHOP


*People just aren't becoming priests. I mean it's not a popular
occupation. Nobody wants to become a priest. It's not a real attractive
job. No pay, no marriage, no fun, just a lot of work.*
CATHOLIC LAYWOMAN

# INTRODUCTION

## THE CHURCH IMPLODES

In the year 2002, the Year of the Pedophile[1] and the fortieth anniversary of the convening of the Second Vatican Council, the Catholic Church in the United States began to implode. The cracks and the fissures and the fractures had been there a long time—inadequate leadership, low quality of service, dissatisfaction with the Vatican, and sex. However, the powerful appeal of the Catholic tradition and the warmth of Catholic community (in some places) held the tottering structure together. The implosion was triggered, as might have been expected, by sex, in this instance the sexual misbehavior of priests and the astonishing attempts by bishops to cover up that misbehavior and subsequently to reassign these priests to parishes where they could continue to abuse children and young people. Many angry Catholic laypeople accused the bishops of protecting the sexual amusements of priests while trying to limit or even eliminate the pleasures of the marriage bed.

The priesthood was under attack. For many months in 2002 newspapers and television reported horrible stories

---

1. In this book I ignore the distinction often made, especially by church people, between pedophilia (abuse of children) and ephebophilia (abuse of adolescent boys). For all practical purposes they are the same. Both result from arrested and twisted sexual development—what Dr. John Money (1968) calls "vandalized love maps." Both are exercises of power over those who are subject to priests or at least inferior in status. The crimes of both should be reported to civil authorities. No one who participates in either type should be reassigned to priestly work.

of the abuse of the young by priests. Rarely did the media suggest that abuse is a widespread problem in the human condition and that clergy of other denominations and other professionals dealing with the young face similar accusations.[2] It seemed that only Catholic priests were abusers and that many, perhaps most, priests were guilty of exploiting defenseless children.

This book is about the Catholic priesthood in the United States during the acute crisis of 2002 and how it fits the stereotypes that emerged at that time and are likely to persist indefinitely. There are not a few ironies in the fire. Forty years ago the Catholic Church was on the front page of all the papers and on the evening news almost every night because of the dramatic and exciting events of the Second Vatican Council. Now it is back on the media radar screen again, this time for disgraceful behavior by priests and even more disgraceful behavior by bishops.

## SEXUAL ABUSE: NOT BANNED IN BOSTON

Many of us who had been warning the Church about sexual abuse thought that the problem had been resolved in the early 1990s.[3] Cardinal Joseph Bernardin of Chicago had established two reform panels, one to comb the files for charges from the past that suggested that a priest had abused children. Twenty-three priests were quietly removed from their parishes. The second panel was a permanent fitness review board composed of priests and a majority of laypeople (with a majority of women) to review preliminary charges against priests and to recommend to the bishop whether a priest ought to be removed from his

---

2. In fact, 17% of Americans were abused before puberty (Laumann and Michaels 1994), equally men and women, and half the men were abused by women.

3. I began warning that sexual abuse was an "atomic bomb ready to explode" in 1985.

work for the protection of children, pending possible criminal action. The system seemed to work well. The cardinal distributed copies of his reform to all the bishops at an annual meeting, and his programs were adopted in many dioceses. Unfortunately they were not adopted in New England.[4]

Early in 2002 during litigation over a particularly nasty case of serial abuse in Boston, Judge Constance M. Sweeney (who had attended Catholic schools for sixteen years) ordered the release of all archdiocesan documents pertaining to the case. They were a treasure trove for the *Boston Globe* and, in short order, for the national media.

Then accusations spread around the country like a smallpox epidemic as past victims finally decided to speak up. Two new elements had been introduced in such charges: civil authorities were much less likely to defer to the Church and keep these cases quiet, and tort lawyers came to realize that there was potential gold in these cases. Most of the accusations were from events in the distant past on which the various statutes of limitations had expired. As Peter Steinfels wrote, very few accusations concerned abuse that had occurred since the widespread implementation of the Chicago reforms. Nonetheless, the sheer horror of the Boston stories captured the imagination of the country. Surveys showed that Catholics were furious, not so much at the abuse as at the cooperation in the abuse by bishops. What else was the reassignment of abusing priests but cooperation?

---

4. Cardinal Bernard Law had elbowed his way ahead of Cardinal Bernardin as the American cardinal with the most clout at the Vatican and did not get along well with the Chicago archbishop. Perhaps Law felt he had nothing to learn from Bernardin. If he had in fact instituted something like the Chicago plan, instead of campaigning against it, he would still have been archbishop of Boston at the end of 2002 and the Church would have been spared a year of self-destruction.

An archbishop and several bishops resigned under charges of being abusers. The diocese of Palm Beach lost two bishops, successively. No one, however, resigned because he had sent an abuser back into a parish.

Bishop Wilton Gregory of Belleville, Illinois, president of the American bishops, did not hesitate to assume leadership.[5] He arranged a meeting of the American cardinals in Rome with the curia and then the pope. He planned a discussion of and vote on draconian measures for dealing with abuse, to take place at a special meeting of bishops in Dallas during June. He delivered a powerful keynote address at the Dallas meeting. His reforms (proposed by a special committee) passed almost unanimously, though some bishops whispered that they were railroaded through the assembly.

The meeting was a media circus as journalists, most of whom lacked the background or training to understand what was happening, tried to collect sound bites from bishops that would explain the reforms and from "victims" who had now cast themselves in the role of the opposition. Around the country the angry and humiliated Catholic laity steamed.

The Dallas protocols were sent off to Rome. Some members of the curial review board (most notably John Baptist Re) supported a two-year approval. Others, more conservative, insisted that there had to be corrections to protect the rights of priests (rights for which the American Civil Liberties Union would have stood in civil law). This Roman caveat (which was relatively minor) created a new tsunami of controversy. By the time the American bishops got

---

5. If he had shown proper concern for his future career, he would not have done so. He is alleged to have offended some powerful American ecclesiastics and some skeptical curialists.

around to trying to explain the matter, the newspaper head-
lines and the CNN summaries had told the country that
the Dallas legislation had been rejected.

A committee of four American cardinals went to Rome
to work out a compromise with the curia. They emerged
satisfied with the restrictions of the Dallas reforms and pro-
claimed the meeting a victory for the Americans. By the
time the text of the agreement had emerged, however, the
American people and especially the livid Catholics had
learned from the media that the American delegation had
caved in. They had not, but they never did manage to
straighten things out.[6]

In general the Vatican behaved badly, that is to say in-
eptly, during the crisis. Curial cardinals tend to be Euro-
pean intellectuals, even if they're South Americans. They
need no evidence and no experience to generalize about the
United States. Thus they argued that it was a local problem
in the United States. They blamed the sexual abuse crisis
on American "pansexualism," on homosexuals, and on the
Jewish media, which were punishing the Church for its support of a Palestinian state. Some of the cardinals whispered
these theories to American journalists. Among the whisper-
ers were men who are deemed to be "papabile," that is,
possible future popes.

Yet the cardinal archbishop of Vienna and the archbishop of Poznań had been forced to retire because of abuse
charges. There were abuse scandals in both Ireland and En-

---

6. The media relations of the American hierarchy were appallingly bad, a
historical problem. A religion writer from a midwestern American paper who
managed to get something right was reprimanded by her editors because her stories did not agree with what was coming from the *New York Times* and the *Washington Post*. If the media managed to perform woefully, one can blame their inex-
perience and perhaps bigotry but more so the failure of the hierarchy to
communicate clearly. In its summary editorial after the Washington special meeting on sexual abuse, the *New York Times* had some of its facts wrong.

gland; the cardinal archbishop of Westminster was at the end of 2002 under investigation by English police for failing to report an abuse charge to the authorities. More scandal news appeared. Several states suspended the statutes of limitations on civil suits so that victims could sue the Church. Two of the most important monasteries in American Catholicism—Gethsemani Abbey in Kentucky (where Thomas Merton had lived) and St. John's Abbey in Minnesota (long-time center of liturgical reform) were rocked by abuse charges.

The last act of the multiple-ring circus took place in autumn at a Washington meeting, when the bishops approved the amended plan. The victim organizations denounced it, as they must denounce everything the Church does, and the media still didn't get it right. The Year of the Pedophile came to an end, as Cardinal Law resigned after Judge Sweeney released yet another pile of incriminating documents; Gallup reported that Catholic church attendance had fallen for the first time below Protestant attendance, and 40% of Catholics said that they might give less money to the Church because of the scandal; and some bishops affirmed that now the time had come for healing and the restoration of trust, an assertion that was even more fatuous than the usual episcopal clichés. Trust patently had to be recovered, not restored; earned, not demanded.

QUADRAGESIMO ANNO

The sexual abuse crisis came after four tumultuous decades caused by the Second Vatican Council.[7] Consider some of

7. *Quadragesimo Anno* (After forty years) is the title of a papal social encyclical written forty years after the first such encyclical in 1892. It's appropriate for a discussion of the problems of the Church in the wake of the Council, which adjourned its first session, having generated enormous hope and excitement, almost forty years to the day before Cardinal Law's resignation.

the facts (cited with relish by that tiny minority of American Catholics who oppose the Council): In 1965 there were 58,000 priests; now there are 45,000. In the 1993 *Los Angeles Times* study of priests (about which more later) the average age of priests was fifty-five. In the 2002 *Times* survey the average age was sixty. In 1965 1,500 priests were ordained, in 2002 450 priests were. In 1965 there were 49,000 seminarians. The number has fallen to 4,700. There were 180,000 nuns; now there are 75,000 and their average age is seventy-two. The Jesuits counted 3,500 seminarians; now they have only 389.

Columnist Patrick Buchanan commented on these facts: "After the opening of Vatican II, reformers were all the rage. They were going to lead us out of our Catholic ghettos by altering the liturgy, rewriting the bible and missals abandoning the old traditions, making us more ecumenical and engaging the world. And their legacy? Four decades of devastation wrought upon the church and the final disgrace of a hierarchy that lacked the moral courage of the Boy Scouts to keep the perverts out of the seminaries and throw them out of the rectories and schools of Holy Mother Church."

Buchanan made two mistakes: Many of the charges that emerged during the Year of the Pedophile were made against men who were ordained before the Second Vatican Council. Nor does he tell us which of the reforms that he opposes caused the apparent collapse of the institutional church—ecumenism, religious liberty, tolerance for Jews, English liturgy? These are reasons why there are fewer seminarians today?

Yet his diatribe is a succinct statement of the position of the Catholic conservatives: the Council destroyed the faith, the Church let homosexuals into its seminaries, and that's why there's an abuse crisis. If the Council hadn't changed anything, none of the losses would have occurred and there would be no abuse crisis.

This is too simple a reading of history and in fact a post-hoc, ergo propter-hoc argument. The reforms of the Council, while not unimportant, were modest attempts at housekeeping by very moderate men. The fathers of the Council broadened the canons of scriptural interpretation, invited other churches and denominations to engage in friendly dialogue, attempted to understand the strengths of the modern world, defended religious freedom, apologized for anti-Semitism, introduced into the lexicon the word "collegiality,"[8] recalled the traditional notion that the Church was not just the hierarchy but the "people of God" including the laity, and approved the translation of the liturgy into vernacular texts. There is no clear connection between any of these changes and the decline in, let us say, vocations to the religious life.

Yet in the decades since 1970 a belief grew among church leaders that it was time at least for a partial "restoration" in which the authority of the hierarchy over the laity and the lower clergy would be enforced again, especially the hierarchy's authority over the sex lives of the laity. Newly appointed bishops would reimpose the rules. Theologians who disagreed would be silenced. Changes would cease. As much as possible, the old order would be restored. Some of the leading progressives of the Council joined the cry for restoration as they became frightened by the chaos and "confusion of the laity" as they saw it.[9] They lost their nerve.

8. Referring primarily to the relationship between the pope and the bishops.

9. Thus Josef Ratzinger, head of the Congregation for the Defense of the Faith (previously called the Holy Office and more previously the Inquisition) changed his mind on five matters he had supported at the Council (where he was an "expert adviser")—liturgical reform, the power of the national conferences of

In these thirty years of attempted restoration, neither the laity nor the lower clergy were won over. Moreover, the hope and elation of the time of the Council turned sour. Priests became bitter at how the curia had ruined their expectations. The "conservatives," lay and clerical, demanded harsh enforcement of the old rules, particularly, as time went on, barring of homosexuals from the priesthood. The "liberals" argued for more democracy in the Church and in particular for the abolition of celibacy and the ordination of women. Both sides grew increasingly angry. Often priests were caught in the middle of conflicts. Then they had to deal with a younger clergy that rejected the Council and all it stood for.

The nonideological laity (the overwhelming majority) were also angry because of the priest shortage, which was growing worse; the authoritarianism of some priests (including the imposition of new—and extracanonical—rules for the reception of the sacraments); the poor quality of preaching and liturgy in local parishes; and the discrimination that they perceived against women (Greeley and Durkin 1984). Priests were in a free-fire zone. Thus, when the second sexual abuse crisis arose in 2002, free-floating anger was widespread in the Church among both laity and lower clergy. The situation was like a huge gasoline leak that needed only a match. Bernard Law, Judge Constance M. Sweeney, and the *Boston Globe* provided the match.

Would the mood have been so sour if Church leadership had been more confident that the Council was the work of the Spirit, and hence more subtle and sophisticated in their

---

bishops, the power of the synod of bishops that meets periodically in Rome, and the reception of Communion by divorced and remarried Catholics. He does not admit he's changed his mind. Nor does he explain why he now criticizes a Council at which he was an important player and where the Holy Spirit was necessarily present, if one believes Catholic teaching.

response to the confusion? Could they have understood that destabilization was inevitable once change had begun and that it was a necessary condition for progress and for the ongoing reform of the Church?

No one knows. The truth is that, given their training and history, most leaders of the Church were quite incapable of such a response even if they had believed it was the correct one. All they could do in a time of crisis was to demand that their authority be recognized just as it had been before the Council.

In this context of anger, disillusion, and bitterness in the Year of the Pedophile, the theories that the problem was either homosexuality or celibacy seemed probable enough. The talking heads who reported what it was like "inside the priesthood" presented plausible arguments. Few priests seemed inclined to argue against the theories. Get rid of celibacy or get rid of the gays, and the abuse will stop.

There is a tradition of research on the priesthood that could provide a very different and more nuanced perspective on the Catholic priesthood in the United States, one in which most people were not interested during the fateful year of 2002 because, like all responsible research, it presents a picture that is gray, ambiguous, problematic, and hence easy to quote out of context and easier to ignore. Reaching back into the late 1960s and extending to an analysis of the 1993 *Los Angeles Times* study of the priesthood (Greeley 1995), it presents priests as on average happy, mature, and self-fulfilled men. I hope that this book contributes to the continuance of that tradition.

In the midst of the sexual abuse crisis of 2002 the *Los Angeles Times* replicated its 1993 survey and added some questions about sexual orientation and practice. The two surveys thus present an excellent opportunity for a "before . . . after" view of a profession under assault. To what extent has the abuse crisis damaged or perhaps even destroyed the morale of the priesthood? Are homosexuality and infidelity rampant in the priesthood? Is celibacy really an insurmountable burden? Are the younger clergy as reactionary as they are thought to be? Are priests really unfulfilled, immature men who would be much better off if they shared a bed with a woman of their own every night?

It is not my intention to mount a defense of the priesthood, though I am now approaching a half century in it. I am well aware of the faults and failings of priests, of the nastiness of clerical culture, of the sloppiness of much clerical performance, of the self-pity that blinded many priests to the abuse problems, even in their own rectories. I began to write about the abuse problem in 1985 (and hence reject the notion that I have no sympathy for victims) and offended most of the priests I had not already offended by reporting on the dissatisfaction of the laity with the professionalism of the clergy, especially with their sermons and liturgy.

Nor is it my intent to argue for the continuation of clerical celibacy. One can make a very good pragmatic case for a change in the celibacy discipline with the argument that it is the only way that the Church can respond to the increasing shortage of priests. Given the demoralization of the Church presently, there may be some reason to suspect that lifting the ban on clerical marriage would actually increase priestly vocations. However, that is not the issue in the present context. The issue is about evidence that celibacy makes priests somehow less than fully human. Must they have experienced sleeping and living with a woman to be sensitive and mature human males?

I hope to report the sociological facts about the Catholic clergy as these facts emerge from analysis of survey data. I doubt that my careful consideration of the data will silence those ideologues (of the right or the left) who have provided raw meat for the feeding frenzy of 2002 without much solid evidence for their assertions.[10] Nor will journalists looking for a two-sentence quote or a twenty-second sound bite find much in the book that will please them.

I will not apologize for using the tools of my trade, statistical tables, significance tests, and graphs. Such tools sometimes infuriate reviewers, who claim that they "mar" a book. If one is doing social science, however, one must use social science tools. The alternative is cocktail chatter, the exchange of opinions and views without the restraints that the logic of social science seeks to impose to achieve a comprehensive and accurate understanding of a phenomenon in a human population.

I am well aware, as is everyone in the survey analysis fraternity, of the limitations of our ways of knowing. Our questions may well be poorly worded, our data collection flawed, our response rates low, our respondents' answers not altogether candid, our interpretations "mired in qualifications," our generalizations, like reality, gray, our interpretative models too simple. Nonetheless, anyone who wishes to talk about a population of human beings has no choice but to ask them questions. Our questions are on the record from the beginning, our samples use the laws of probability, our methods require us to stick closely to our data sets and to be clear when we go beyond the data, our generalizations are qualified by the diversity that appears in the data, our recommendations are carefully distinguished from the data, if based to some extent on them.

Our way of knowing is not that of strong opinions in faculty lounges, dinner-party discussions, bar talk, tête-à-têtes with old acquaintances, conversations with family and

10. Richard Sipe (1990, 1992) will tell you how many Catholic bishops in the world are gay, but he won't tell you how he knows.

friends, "balanced" feature stories and news reports, and quotes from our favorite columnists. Our way of knowing is less than perfect but, when skillfully carried out, more precise most of the time than most other ways of knowing.

I thus approach this research exercise with an open mind and an empiricist's hunger for evidence.[11] The only expectation that I have from previous research, and this is a very tentative expectation, is that priests are a mixed lot (as is every other group of human beings) and that on the whole they are not nearly as immature, frustrated, unhappy, and sexually deprived or depraved as they were alleged to be during the Year of the Pedophile.

Whenever I finish a book like this one, I am acutely aware of its imperfections—low response rate, dubious questions, limitations imposed by the questionnaire on further analyses, the dryness of survey descriptions, the monotony of repeated %s, unsatisfactory attempts to write for both sociologists and laity. I also am conscious of the general limitations of sociology and my own particular limitations. I say to myself, "This isn't a very good book." Usually it isn't very good. Usually, however, it is the best there is on the subject, because it is the only one of its kind.

Until someone comes along with more resources (and perhaps more skills) to do a better empirical book on the Catholic priesthood in the United States—and I hope that happens soon—this imperfect volume will have to be the best there is.

*Chicago*
*Feast of All the Souls in Purgatory 2002.*[12]

11. In the interest of full disclosure I am a heterosexual celibate, happy in the priesthood, and with no intention of leaving, not even if (when) they try to drive me out.
12. Aka Day of the Dead and Sahmain.

# 1

## INSIDE THE "SECRET WORLD"

In this chapter I will review the work of those who have tried to explain to the American public, through their access to the media, the "inside" of celibate Catholic priesthood, to tear away the veil behind which priests have so long hidden their secret fantasies and vices. Their theories converge with the beliefs of many Americans who are not Catholic and have always been suspicious of a celibate priesthood. These theories also shaped the media approach to the Year of the Pedophile as journalists looked for informed experts they could quote. They stand as the conventional wisdom about priests, which currently permeates American society. It is precisely this conventional wisdom I wish to examine against my data.

### WHY ABUSE?

Why did this abuse happen? Most of those who spoke to the media or wrote on the subject assumed that the reason was obvious. Priests could not marry, either because of church law or because they were incapable of mature sexual love with a woman. Therefore they preyed on the young and innocent. The only way to stop the abuse was to eliminate the foolish celibacy rule and with it the sinister clerical culture that supported abusers. For Catholic "liberals" the abuse scandal provided a rallying point to push their demands for a married clergy, women priests, and a more democratic church.

Catholic conservatives saw the crisis as the result of the changes in the Church instituted in the wake of the Second Vatican Council. They blamed abuse on homosexual priests, on the clergy's tolerance of sexual deviation, and on the failure of priests to preach the Catholic birth-control ban. Editorial writers and columnists (some, like Maureen Dowd, Bill Keller, and Jimmy Breslin, with a thin connection to the Church) denounced priests and the Church for their medieval, antisex ideology of celibacy.

The pressure on the priesthood was unremitting—a new scandal almost every day, a new denunciation of celibacy or homosexuality. The talking heads on TV and the "experts" quoted in the print media rarely spoke out in defense of priests. Those priests who did appear on the various TV talk programs seemed incoherent or self-righteous or worried about the decline in their own personal image. The priest organizations around the country seemed to be more concerned about false accusations than about the abuse of children and minors.

Occasionally someone observed that abusers of the young were usually men with deep and perhaps incurable personality problems and that, if they marry, they often abuse their own children. Marriage then does not seem to be a cure for abuse. Almost no one said that it degraded women to assume that the abolition of celibacy would stop abuse. Rarely someone argued that most priests were not abusers and that not only priests abuse. The scandal tidal wave had taken over. The defining paradigm of abuse and cover-up dominated the story till the end of the year.

Journalists sought out "experts," mostly former priests, to answer their questions. Some former priests hinted that those who remain in the priesthood are not real men because they do not sleep with a woman. They spoke of the infantilism of the male clerical culture, which produced and protected abusers. They questioned the psychological maturity of priests, and their fidelity to the promise of celibacy. One former priest argued that only 2% of priests are "mature celibates" (whatever that may mean) and provided a detailed analysis of the sexual problems of the other 98%. No one seemed to wonder whether the comments of such men might be just a little self-serving.

These "experts" were not widely known in the Catholic population and had little influence in general on Catholic thinking—though most priests have heard about them. However, they used their fifteen minutes of celebrity to reinforce the general assumption among Americans that celibacy is unhealthy and that it was no surprise that celibates are freaks, and perhaps monsters.

For American priests these attacks, which had begun in the early nineties and then subsided till the Boston scandals of the Year of the Pedophile, were a new experience. They had grown up in a cultural environment in which priests were admired and respected. The celibate priest was a folk hero (Bing Crosby, Pat O'Brien, Spencer Tracy, James Cagney, even Frank Sinatra). People deferred to him, tipped their hat to him, smiled at him, gave him discounts in stores. Now everyone seemed to hold him in contempt. Yet most priests felt that they had done nothing to deserve such a change in response. They were unaware that in the literature of France, Spain, Italy, and Portugal, the priest is often a creepy villain. Nor did they have any memory of the awful days of the *Awful Disclosures of Maria Monk* (1850) and the assault on the idea of a celibate priesthood by anti-Catholic nativism in the nineteenth century. For that matter, neither did anyone in the media seem aware of that remnant of the anti-Catholic past and wonder whether it might be contributing to the feeding frenzy.

Priests often found themselves criticized by their lay parishioners who were dissatisfied with the clergy's exercise of professional skills—only half as likely as Protestants to rate their performance excellent. In addition Catholic "conservatives" were arguing that a large proportion of priests, perhaps half, were gay. Catholic "liberals" were lamenting the fact that the more recently ordained clergy (not necessarily younger because of the large number of "belated" vocations) were conservatives, even to the extent of appearing in old-fashioned garb like cassocks and birettas. Finally, many parishes were surviving with only one priest and perhaps a pastor emeritus and one or two foreign student priests.

It was not an easy time to be a priest.

In this chapter I will consider different portraits of the priesthood, three of which largely shape the public images of priests—the work of Eugene Cullen Kennedy, A. W. Richard Sipe, Peter McDonough, and Eugene Bianchi. I will note the demographic contribution of the late Richard Schoenherr and the theoretical conclusions he drew from his findings. I will also consider the work of Thomas Nestor, who presents a very different picture. Kennedy and Sipe are psychologists, McDonough and Bianchi are sociologists, as was Schoenherr. Nestor is a psychologist. Kennedy, Sipe, and Bianchi are "inactive" priests, Nestor is still a priest in the "active ministry," Schoenherr left the active ministry in 1972.

### EUGENE CULLEN KENNEDY

If one is to analyze the maturity and sexuality of priests, two canons ought to be observed. First, the sample of priests studied should represent a valid mirror of the whole priesthood. Second, comparison, the normal tool of social science, should be used in analysis. Thus if one says that priests lack a healthy capacity for intimacy, one should be careful that the respondents are chosen in such a way that one might validly generalize from their skills at intimacy to the whole population of priests and that the intimate skills of priests are less than those of the general population of males or the general population of married males, of the same educational backgrounds and age as the priests. Should a clinician judge from his work in therapy that priests are not capable of intimacy, he must persuade us that the priests he has treated accurately reflect the condition of the priesthood and that their low level of skill in intimate behavior is worse than that of comparable married men.

The simple statement that priests are sexually immature thus raises the question, relative to whom? Who among us can claim to be sexually mature? Who indeed among the clinicians who appoint themselves judges of the sexual immaturity of others can claim to be sexually mature? In matters of the capacity for intimacy and sexual maturity, it often seems that the human species has hardly progressed beyond late adolescence.

Eugene Cullen Kennedy has been writing about the psychology of the priesthood for forty years. His principle research study appeared in 1972 (Kennedy and Heckler 1972) as part of a multidisciplinary study of the priesthood funded by the National Conference of Catholic Bishops at that time.[1] Kennedy and a team of psychologists at Loyola University engaged in clinical interviews with a sample of 271 Catholic priests who were chosen from the sample es-

1. The entire project included work by historians, psychologists, social activists, and sociologists. Part of it was a study by the National Opinion Research Center (NORC). Since the NORC study included three separate surveys—priests, bishops, and former priests—it was the most expensive. This fact occasioned some unfavorable comment among critics and perhaps some envy among other scholars. The implication was that I was making money on the project. In fact, none of the funding for the NORC study went to pay my salary.

tablished by the National Opinion Research Center (NORC 1972) for the sociological study the bishops had also commissioned. Through interviews and tests and independent evaluations the Loyola team divided 224 of these respondents into four categories—developed ($n = 19$); developing ($n = 50$); underdeveloped ($n = 139$); and mal-developed ($n = 16$). The authors assert that no claim concerning population proportions is intended. Yet one wonders why not. If in some sense the sample is drawn from a probability sample of American priests, one should be able to make at least rough estimates from the sample to the population. Hence one might conclude that half the priests in the country are emotionally "underdeveloped" and only 14% are "developed." The description of these "ideal types" is followed by case histories illustrative of each group.

The authors say that priests are "ordinary" men, no better and no worse than other males. In fact the "underdeveloped" and the "mal-developed" seem to have serious personality problems, especially in areas of religious faith and celibacy.[2] Either the priests whom the team interviewed are typical and most priests are not emotionally developed, or they are not typical and the only point of the exercise is to provide interesting, useful, and sometimes melancholy information.

Much of the analysis compares the four groups. While the sampling may be adequate for the type of study intended, there are no norms by which the members of the sample can be compared to other men. Hence we cannot judge whether a priestly vocation and celibacy contribute to disproportionate emotional immaturity among priests.

---

2. The case histories are often written in the supercilious tone that some psychologists adopt when speaking of their patients. Granting that all professions are entitled to their own rhetoric, the implicit superiority in the psychological tone can be infuriating.

When a layperson (a laywoman perhaps) complains about the immaturity of priests on the basis of an experience with a priest, one can understand her dismay, but question (in one's own head) whether she can validly generalize to all priests on the basis of a single case, any more than she might claim that all men are predators on the basis of an encounter with a single male predator (or several thereof).

Norms were available to make such a comparison in the Loyola research. At Loyola's recommendation NORC distributed to a subsample of priests a psychological instrument called the Personality Orientation Inventory (POI), developed by Shostrom (1963), which purports to measure nine dimensions of "self-actualization" as described by Maslow (1962), including one that measures a "capacity for intimacy." Indeed, responding to the POI was one of the norms for falling into the Loyola sample. Thus it should have been possible to compare priests with various norm groups that the POI had established. However, the Loyola team did not attempt such comparisons. Therefore, nothing in their report enables one to make judgments about the relative "self-actualization" of priests.

In chapter 3 of the NORC sociological report (1972) priests were compared with groups for which norms were available.[3] On none of the nine scales—including the capacity for intimacy—were priests significantly lower than age peers. Hence there was no support for the position that priesthood and celibacy affect either self-actualization or capacity for intimacy or any of the other seven scales one can create from the POI.

---

3. The NORC sample was a multistaged random probability sample. Primary sampling units were dioceses and religious orders, weighted by size. Within these units individual respondents were chosen by random probability. Mail questionnaires were sent to more than 5,000 priests with three follow-up mailings and a phone interview with nonrespondents. The final effective response rate was 71%.

The POI results show no appreciable differences between priests and laymen in their age category on measures of self-actualization. Young priests, for example, score higher on the self-actualization scales than college students, and compare favorably with Peace Corps volunteers.

The results show a slight relationship between an "inner-directed" personality score and a propensity to resign from the priesthood. However, it appears that there is a tendency for the latter to be hyperactualized, and for those who remain to be hypoactualized. In other words, some of those who leave the priesthood show excessive need for independence, and some of those who stay show excessive need for dependence, which suggests that some men leave because they are overactualized and some men stay because they are underactualized. It must be noted, however, that the overwhelming majority of those who score high on the self-actualization measures remain in the priesthood.

The POI results give no evidence for the frequent assertion that priests have passive-dependent personalities. The indication is that one of the principal emotional deficiencies of priests is a tendency to be less able than others to cope with aggressive feelings; in other words, the priest is, if anything, more passive aggressive than passive dependent. If he has any tendency in passive directions, it is to control others by his passivity. His neurotic style, when it exists, is more likely to be that of the "nice guy" rather than that of the dependent child.

The POI also indicated special strengths in the priesthood. It would appear that priests are relatively stronger than other groups in their ability to affirm their own self-worth and to accept themselves for what they are in spite of weaknesses and deficiencies.

There is no indication that those who entered the seminary later or who had more postordination educational experience score any higher on measures of self-actualization than other priests. Neither is there any evidence to indicate that the clergy are any more deficient than comparable groups in their capacity for intimate friendships.

Finally, there is no evidence that the priesthood has attracted men whose social class, family background, or childhood experiences have made them less likely to be autonomous than the typical American male.

The Loyola team wrote that priests were "ordinary." NORC concluded, on the basis of personality measures that the Loyola team had recommended but not used, that priests were in general "not different from other males." These conclusions are not quite the same. "Ordinary" means not better than anyone else. "Not different" means not inferior psychologically to anyone else, despite their seminary training and their celibate commitments.

One might have expected the NORC findings to have been definitive. However, those who argued to the special emotional immaturity of priests solved that problem by simply ignoring the findings.

Kennedy subsequently left the active priesthood[4] but continued to write books, articles, and op-ed columns in oracular and sometimes purple prose (the sexual abuse crisis was the iceberg that cut into the hull of the Titanic of the "asexual church") about the psychological deficiencies of celibate priests. Celibacy has created an asexual clerical culture, he often argues, a culture that impedes emotional development, reinforces a patriarchal caste in which some men dominate all other men and abusers can easily hide. This "asexual culture" is the Church's persistent sexual wound.

Because Kennedy has had psychological training and ex-

4. A humiliating process, as he describes in Kennedy 2001.

perience, because he treated priests in therapy, and because he directed the Loyola study, his assertions enjoy some credibility. However, his sweeping generalizations are personal opinions, if informed personal opinions, and very little else. Yet he is an "expert," a talking head who helps shape media spin on the Catholic priesthood.

The "sexual wound" that he describes in these generalizations may have been in the process of healing since the early 1970s, when the lower clergy and the laity in great numbers agreed to disagree with the Vatican on sexual matters (Greeley 2003). Now lay Catholics on the average engage in intercourse and in sexual experimentation and sexual play more often than Protestants and are more willing to tolerate homosexuals.

It is, in Kennedy's opinion, the "asexual clerical culture" that is responsible for the sexual abuse crisis. Celibacy may not cause men to be molesters, but clerical culture is a place where they could hide and be confident that it would shelter them and deny their guilt.

One may dislike clerical culture intensely (I do) and still wonder about such a general cultural analysis. Social science research is wary of this mode of analysis because it explains too much. *Qui nimis probat, nihil probat* (one who proves too much, proves nothing), as the dictum of the Schoolmen put it. It is certainly true that priests tend to protect other priests. It is also true that in this respect bishops are priests. The policy of dissimulation and denial in the sexual abuse cases was the result of such misplaced (and evil) loyalty. However, many other professional groups engage in similar loyalty-motivated behavior—doctors, politicians, police, and the military, for example—without needing to add clerical celibacy to the explanatory model. It is true that the person whose "love maps," as Money (1968) calls them, incline them to seek out children or minors as their preferred sexual partner experience a certain safety if they are celibate clergy. However, other predators hide successfully in professions that work with children, like education and coaching.

Thus Kennedy's analysis of the evils of celibacy, as vivid as it may be, seems to reach too far. The NORC findings about the psychological condition of celibate priests reported in 1972 still stand.

## A. W. RICHARD SIPE

A. W. Richard Sipe (1990), like Kennedy an inactive and married priest and a psychologist, accepts the validity of the NORC analysis for its time, but argues that since then there has been a "sexual revolution" and that the NORC conclusions are therefore out of date. Contributing to this "revolution," he argues, were the increase in sexual explicitness, the works of Kinsey and Masters and Johnson, the publication of *Playboy*, the emergence of the women's rights and the gay movement, the AIDS epidemic, the emphasis on androgyny, and the development of oral contraceptives. In such a context, the meaning of clerical celibacy has changed.

Such an agglomeration of cultural forces certainly indicates change. Whether the word "revolution" is appropriate is another question. Were men and women, especially younger men and women, drawn more intensely to one another after 1960? Reading of fiction and poetry from earlier eras might make one doubt it. Was there more tolerance for extramarital and gay sex after 1960? Did young people engage in more interactions that would lead to orgasm after 1960? Have the frequency rates of marital sex increased in recent decades? Has sexual pleasure and fulfillment increased? Have priests found women more attractive than in times past?

The answers to these questions are surely problematic. Tom Smith of NORC (1999) has contended, based on an examination of data, that the principal changes in sexual behavior have come from the development of oral contraceptives and the resulting lowering of the age of a person's first sexual activity and the increasing number of sexual partners one has before marriage. However, the age of first sexual encounter has diminished by only a year and the number of sexual partners has increased by only one. Disapproval of extramarital sex remains constant, though more recently toleration of homosexual sex has increased.

Robert Michael (1988) has argued that divorce rates have increased because of a combination of oral contraceptives and new employment possibilities for women. Laumann et al. (1994) report that rates of extramarital sex are surprisingly low and the highest level of sexual satisfaction exists among permanently committed partners.

In summary the sexual revolution might well be reduced to technology—the development of relatively safe and relatively effective contraceptives, especially the birth-control pill.

When one considers the sexual revolution in these specific and concrete circumstances, one must ask, has it added to the primal attraction that draws men and women together, save perhaps in some peripheral matters? Has celibacy become any more difficult than it once was? Do priests find the appeal of women any more compelling than they did, let us say, in the time of St. Augustine—who was obsessed by that appeal?

The answers to those questions are not immediately apparent. Hence Sipe's attempt to make the problems of celibate priests different after 1965 than they were before 1965 because of the "sexual revolution" ought to be considered cautiously.

He tells us that he is engaged in "search" rather than "research" (8), though it is not clear exactly what he means. He does not have a valid sample from which to generalize to the whole population of priests. His "sample" involves "approximately" 1,500 priests, a third of whom he has talked to in clinical interviews. "Another third of the informants were clergy who were not patients but who share information during meetings, interviews and consultations both individually and in small groups." The final third were those who "knew about the behavior of priests—sexual partners, victims, or otherwise direct observers of it."

All of these materials are interesting, and Sipe makes good use of them in telling his story of the "secret world" of clerical celibacy. If he had been content to do that, one could have accepted his book without criticism as a description of some of the pathologies to be found among priests. However, Sipe claims in the book and in many public interviews to have derived from his sample accurate and precise numbers in the various categories of homosexual and heterosexual priestly behavior—about 2% are "successfully celibate," for example. He may well be right that the sexual revolution has changed the condition of celibacy in the priesthood since the NORC report of 1972. But he has not proved his point and could have proved it only if he replicated the POI with a representative sample of American priests. In the absence of a replication, the reader will just have to take his word for it.

As it is, much of the book, unsurprisingly given the nature of Sipe's sampling techniques, is about pathology. It makes for melancholy reading, but doubtless has persuaded many (including fellow clinician Jack Dominian, who writes about such matters for the British Catholic periodical the *Tablet*) that it is an accurate picture of the priesthood. Need one say that those encountered in clinical situations are hardly reflective of a larger population, no matter who the members of that population might be?

Recently he has, according to public reports, offered precise numbers about homosexual bishops. Without adequate sampling techniques, only God could make such estimates. The only sample that is useful to make valid estimates for a population is a probability sample, that is, one in which every time a respondent to be sampled is selected, every other person in the population has an equal chance of falling into the sample.[5] Anyone who has completed an advanced undergraduate course in elementary statistics knows that this is the only way to do it. Any other form of sampling is worthless. The acronym GIGO—garbage in, garbage out—applies to Sipe's sample. As a clinician he probably did not have a course in statistical inference. Yet it is hard to excuse his blithe disregard for elementary methodology. He is patently very proud of his long years of experience and hard work in interviewing priests, and with some reason. Yet because he cites precise numbers, there is a touch of charlatanry in his estimates. If he had resisted the temptation to generalize from his sample, his book would have been interesting and useful. However, it would not have captured the media attention that his precise numbers guarantee. When the subject is the Catholic clergy, the media couldn't care less about the rules of statistical inference. Yet it is unthinkable that journalists would predict outcomes of elections by such methods.

Nor does Sipe's work meet the second desideratum mentioned at the beginning of this chapter. He offers no

5. Sipe is not the only Catholic writer who acts as if probability samples are not necessary. Many priests, nuns, and laity assume that while "NORC-type samples"—as they call them—are certainly high quality, other, less perfect samples can still be useful, especially if they are large enough. Unfortunately one cannot by good intentions and hard work repeal the rules of statistical inference.

comparison of priests with married men of comparable age and educational background. What proportion of married men would measure in as "successful married lovers" by standards similar to those which Sipe uses for "successful celibacy"? If 2% of priests are pedophiles (a low estimate in my judgment), what percentage of married adult males are sexual predators?[6]

In Sipe's second book (1995), he argues, apparently in response to critiques of his methodology, that he "has indulged in guerilla research that has a long history, noble tradition, and productive track record." Fair enough, if he is putting together a life-long history of experiences and impressions. But he has no right to assign precise estimates to the population of priests based on such guerilla activity, precise estimates that he has freely quoted to journalists. At that point, as a purported depiction of the population, guerilla research becomes garbage research.

Sipe's books are not only wrong-headed, despite his apparent sincerity and integrity; they are in fact very dangerous. One might well be inclined to call them defamatory. His "secret world" is not the real world. It is a world of guesswork, some of it perhaps shrewd, but guesswork just the same, masquerading as serious and responsible social science.

## PETER MCDONOUGH
## AND EUGENE BIANCHI

Peter McDonough and Eugene Bianchi (2001) are the most recent additions to the ranks of those who are willing and able to tell what it's like inside the "secret world" of the Catholic clergy. In their case it is the world inside the Soci-

6. Laumann et al. (1994) report that 17% of Americans have been sexually abused before puberty.

ety of Jesus, to which Bianchi once belonged. Their data are based on "snowball" samples of 226 Jesuits and 204 former Jesuits: an interviewee is asked if he could recommend someone else who might be willing to talk to the interviewer, even if that person disagrees with the interviewee. There are few tabulations in *Passionate Uncertainty*. Rather, excerpts from the interviews are used to illustrate themes from McDonough's and Bianchi's overarching theories of the plight of the Jesuits—and by extension the priesthood and the Church.

Their thesis seems to be that the Society of Jesus in the United States is in a serious and possibly terminal crisis. The present situation is the result of the turning away from the Church's sexual ethic after the Second Vatican Council, the decline in vocations, the "autocratic populism" of the Vatican, and replacement of Jesuits by laymen in Jesuit institutions. Men survive in the society by private dissent from the Vatican, a "therapeutic spirituality," and a congeries of "countercultures"—a variety of ministries that have not been part of the Jesuit tradition.

It is difficult to know whether this perspective existed before their research and was confirmed by it or whether it flowed out of research findings. One finds it hard to escape the conclusion that the findings are shaped by the perspective instead of shaping it. McDonough and Bianchi, both with long experience of Jesuits, must have had a pretty clear notion of what the society's problems were before they began their interviews.

They defend their sampling methodology as the only one possible and, in response to reviews, as the best method of studying the Jesuits. But it is certainly not the only one possible, at least for a study of those still in the society, because there is no reason why they could not have interviewed a random probability sample of those who remain

Jesuits. Moreover, it is absurd to argue that it is the best kind of sample. The built-in biases of such snowball samples are obvious: respondents are likely to nominate other respondents who share their own views, despite the interviewers' statement that this is not a necessary condition. The respondents may be typical of Jesuits, but there is no compelling social science reason for concluding that they are.

Moreover there is a bias in comparing those who have left the society with those who remain in it. The former have achieved some closure of their problems with the priesthood or the society, and the latter have not. The former are generally at peace with their decisions, the latter remain inside a situation in which most experience some tension. Hence it is easy for the authors to engage in often patronizing explanations of how those who remain have come to terms with their tensions by various psychological mechanisms. If you are persuaded by your theories that the society is in terminal distress, you will tend to suspect that those who remain in it are to some extent rationalizing their decisions. Therefore you must discipline yourself with a far more sophisticated methodology than the authors display. There is no way to be sure that the authors, for all their sophisticated manipulation of social science theory and terminology, are not making a pilgrimage from preconceived bias to foregone conclusion.

I know many Jesuits. My impression is that by and large they are happy and fulfilled men. I could just as reasonably generalize from my encounters to the society, as McDonough and Bianchi do from their interviews. I do not do so, because the rules of the game say that you don't make estimates unless you have representative samples.

RICHARD SCHOENHERR

The late Richard Schoenherr was an inactive priest and a professor of sociology at the University of Wisconsin who for thirty years engaged in (accurate) projections of the decline of the number of priests in the United States because of resignation and declining vocations. His analysis (1993) is sound and one of the best demographic portraits of any profession ever constructed.

His colleagues published after his death an edited version of a massive book on which he had been working for years (Schoenherr 2002), in which he provided a theoretical explanation for the decline of the priesthood. In his view the hegemonic all-male, celibate priesthood was an instrument in the maintenance of the male, patriarchal structure of the Catholic Church. The second book is not, strictly speaking, a sociological exercise; it is a theoretical perspective from which to view his data. Schoenherr's work therefore is not like that of the writers discussed previously, who were uninhibited by data or careful analysis.

While the second book is based on the first, it does not follow from it inexorably. It is clear from the work of Chaves (1999) that the married clergy of the Protestant denominations are patriarchal and that even when women are admitted into the ministry they often acquire little or no real power in the denomination. The ordination of married men or of women would not, if the example of the Protestant denominations tells us anything, eliminate Catholic patriarchy or necessarily change it all that much.

Nonetheless, Schoenherr's predictions about declining numbers of priests have been remarkably accurate. Yet there is no sign that Catholic leaders are thinking seriously about a future only a decade away when there will be many fewer priests and many more angry laity demanding more priests in their parishes.

## THOMAS NESTOR

The Loyola University doctoral dissertation of Thomas Nestor is unusual not only because he is an active priest but because he studied a valid probability sample of priests (of the archdiocese of Chicago) and compared them to married men of the same age and educational background. No one has paid much attention to his work, which is not surprising because his findings present a different picture of the priesthood than the one made popular by the preceding authors. Indeed, his findings are like those reported in the 1972 NORC report.

Nestor addressed himself to the question of "intimacy and adjustment" in priests. His summary is worth quoting at some length (1993, 122).

> The results of the present study suggest that regardless of the general deficiencies that men show in intimate relationships, priests were more likely to enter into close relationships than their male peers. The priests experienced significantly higher levels of intimacy in their relationships than other men. While some of this difference can probably be attributed to the wider exposure of the priests to potential relationships and potential intimacy in the exercise of their ministry, the data indicated nonetheless that priests regard a larger number of people as close friends upon whom they can rely and in whom they can confide. The priests were more likely to count on these important others for support and acceptance than other men did in their lives. In addition, the priests demonstrated more eagerness to enter into relationships of varying depths and they reported that they enjoy providing support, nurturance, care, and concern to others more than other men did.

On all of the dimensions of intimacy examined in this study, the priests were either significantly better equipped than the controls for close relationships or, at least, were equal to the controls in the practice of engaging, developing, and sustaining close relationships.

It is important to note that on the Miller Social Intimacy Scale, which measures, among other things, the readiness priests demonstrated for expression of affection, self disclosure, and closeness to significant other, the priests were as intimate as the married and single men who comprised the control group. The Miller Social Intimacy Scale taps some behaviors, for example, professions of affection, which are more commonly found in married subjects than unmarried subjects. Despite the instrument's apparent bias in favor of married people, there were no significant differences between the priests, all of whom were single, and the controls, eighty percent of whom were married, in their level of social intimacy.

Nestor also reported that priests were higher than the control groups on measures of work satisfaction and life satisfaction. Thus, while Kennedy reported that priests were "ordinary," Nestor's conclusions could be paraphrased as indicating that priests were better than ordinary.

Despite Sipe's claim that the "sexual revolution" had changed the condition of priests since the NORC 1972 report, Nestor's evidence suggests continuity rather than change. It is most unfortunate that those currently pontificating about the priesthood have not considered his work.

## CONCLUSION

Some of the authors discussed above are inactive and married Catholic priests. Whatever their intentions in writing about the culture of those they left behind in the priesthood, they can hardly escape a bit of suspicion that their work is self-justifying, that they are saying to those who have remained priests that they lacked the courage to follow them in their departure from the priesthood or are sustaining the hegemony of an all-male, patriarchal church. This posture, while not common, is not completely absent from those who have resigned from the active ministry. In effect their message could easily be interpreted as "we are the men of virtue and vision because we had the courage to leave that vipers' tangle of sickness and become honest and free." Or as the *New York Times* quoted an inactive priest who is a psychologist, "the healthy ones began to jump ship."

Why is it not enough merely to resign and get on with one's life? Why must they continue to justify their decision by questioning the opposite decision others might have made? Why fight the old battles with a clerical culture you found oppressive and left in search of freedom and maturity?

It is not an easy task to leave the priesthood. One faces crises with one's family, one's colleagues, one's people. It is a harsh and painful break with a life that in many ways was satisfying. Moreover, the Vatican is cruel—a word that is not excessive—in its treatment of those who wish to leave the priesthood and to marry and remain in the Church in good standing. It is hard to understand why Church leaders cannot extend gratitude for years of service and good wishes for the rest of the man's life. In its present style, however, the leadership seems determined to humiliate and torment him. Minimally there's not much trace of the compassion of the Gospels in such behavior.[7] One can hardly blame Kennedy, for example, for his fury at the way

7. As I have said, I have no intention of ever leaving the priesthood. Indeed, I won't go even if they try to get rid of me—always a possibility. However, I reflect on occasion that the Church's rules for resigning priests are so cruel as arguably to be invalid.

he was humiliated by the Vatican. Assaulting the celibate priesthood could easily be the result of pain and anger.

Arguably the authors cited in this review of the literature are motivated by a desire to help reform in a church about which they are still deeply concerned. However, it is not the task of a sociologist to assess the motives of others. I merely note the anger and the ultimate incompetence of their assaults. Make no mistake about it, the work of these authors is fatally flawed social science. Their books and articles purport to tell the "inside story" of celibate immaturity in the priesthood. They fail to do so because of inadequate sample design and the absence of comparison with married men.

Is it not unfair, however, to apply the norms of social science to their books? Are they not merely collecting their own impressions, telling their own stories, reporting on their own anguished experiences? If that were all they were attempting, no one could fault them. In fact, however, they are attempting much more. Each in his own way is trying to reveal what the celibate life of priests is like from the inside by using his skills as a psychologist or a sociologist.

The thoughtful reader who is not a social scientist may well wonder how typical are the priests to whom or about whom the authors have talked and whether they are on average more inadequate as mature men than those who are not priests. My contention in previous work and in this volume is not that priests are paragons of maturity and personal well-being, but that they are not dissimilar from married laymen of comparable educational background.

The works of most of these authors, however, neatly convey the conventional wisdom before and during the Year of the Pedophile about the dysfunctions of a celibate priesthood. It is against the data collected in the two *Los Angeles Times* studies that this wisdom must be tested.

# 2

## SEXUAL ORIENTATION
## AND CELIBACY

The *Los Angeles Times* has surveyed representative samples of priests twice by mail in the last decade, in the autumn of 1993 (2,064 respondents) and in the summer and autumn of 2002 (1,854 respondents).[1] The appendix provides a statement of the methodology the *Times* used, a copy of the questionnaire, cover letters, and follow-up mailings.[2] In both years there were strong objections in some Catholic quarters to the study. It was assumed that, if a prominent national media outlet was doing a survey of priests, it was

1. The 2002 project began after the bishops conference in Dallas in June at which the documents on sexual abuse were approved and ended before their conference in Washington in November when they revised some of the Dallas norms at the request of the Vatican.

2. The appendix describes the methodology of the *Times* survey. It is regrettable that the response rate was not higher. The *Times* researchers considered it comparable to their ordinary political and election studies. At NORC we would have demanded a rate twice as high. As one colleague remarked, "You want the gold standard while they provided the industry standard." One works with what one has. As we shall see later, the crucial findings on the morale of priests were replicated in a NORC study with a 73% response rate—a fact that notably enhances confidence in the *Los Angeles Times* data. One can also create models that make certain assumptions about those who do not respond. Sixteen percent of the *Times* respondents said that they were homosexual in their orientation. If one assumes that the nonrespondents were twice as likely to be homosexuals, then the real homosexual rate would be 24%. If, on the other hand, the nonrespondents were only half as likely to be homosexual, the real homosexual rate would be only 12%.

Critics of the sample are free, of course, to collect their own sample. Critics of the analysis are equally free to reanalyze the *Times* data themselves.

doing so to foster an attack on the priesthood.[3] In 2002 these objections persisted even though the reports of the 1993 study were favorable to the priesthood.

There are three advantages in working with the *Times* data.[4] (1) The nine years that separated the two surveys were an era in which the sexual abuse crisis became national news. Hence one can measure the impact, if any, of the crisis on priests. (2) They are the first two studies done by an agency that is not Catholic since the 1970 NORC study of priesthood (NORC 1972). Hence they provide opportunities for some measures over time of the condition of the priesthood in the United States. The similarity reported in chapter 1 between NORC measures of emotional maturity and capacity for intimacy among priests and those of Thomas Nestor suggests that the 1970 research might still be relevant.[5] (3) The second *Times* survey is the first

3. Thus William Donahue of the Catholic League for Religious and Civil Rights (in the December 2002 issue of the newsletter *Catalyst*) attacked the survey because of some of the questions, such as "When you need counsel and guidance, how comfortable do you feel about going to your bishop or to the superiors of your order?" *Catalyst* quotes with approval a priest as saying that the question is "ridiculous. It is just not a reality that priests go to their bishop for counsel since they have personal spiritual directors and it is not practical especially in large dioceses." In fact, 70% of priests said they would feel comfortable with such a contact. Donahue, who is a sociologist, also asserts that the second mailing, standard practice in all mail surveys, was sent because "they got stiffed" the first time around. It is unlikely that Donahue will take a more charitable view of this book.

4. The major disadvantage is that the response rate, while satisfactory from the perspective of the *Times*, is not what a NORC researcher would like and even normally demand. One works with what one has.

5. The 1970 research was part of a larger, allegedly multidisciplinary study of the priesthood. It was commissioned by the American bishops, one suspects in retrospect, as a delaying action. They found themselves under pressure from their clergy and laity for more changes such as those instituted by the Second Vatican Council. They argued that they must undertake a study first to find out what the actual situation was. Perhaps they expected that research would reveal that the Church and the priesthood were more stable than some claimed. In fact, the study found many positive aspects in the lives of priests. However, it also

time that a national sample of priests have been asked directly about their sexual behavior.

Whether they answered truthfully or not may be another question. It has been our experience at NORC that people tend to answer questions about their sexual behavior with candor, as long as they are assured of anonymity. Moreover, the priests who filled out the questionnaire could have simply refused to answer the questions about sexual orientation and behavior.

The only way one can find data about sexual orientation and the practice of celibacy is by asking people questions. A national-sample survey has the merit of asking a large number of people in clearly defined items. It does not rely on vague impressions or on dubious generalizations from clinical encounters or dinner-party conversations to a large population.

## SEXUAL ORIENTATION
### AND SEXUAL BEHAVIOR

The first question about sexuality in the 2002 *Times* study (question 55) is "Some people think of themselves as heterosexual in orientation, while others think of themselves as homosexual in orientation and still others feel their sexual orientation lies somewhere in between. How about you?" Seventy percent replied that they were heterosexual,

---

discovered strong dissent about certain Catholic sexual teachings (birth control and masturbation, for example). The bishops thereupon tried to discredit the study and to distance themselves from it. Three sociologists were commissioned to review the work, and their critique was to be bound into the published book— without the authors of the book having an opportunity to respond. (The major criticism of the reviewers was that a survey ought not to have been used, which ignored the fact that surveys are what NORC does.) When this dirty trick was defeated, they did the next best thing: they established a committee to study the NORC report—a surefire technique in the world of the Catholic hierarchy to bury unpleasant facts. So the NORC report, unread and unseen for the most part, pleased no one, though no one ever refuted any of its findings.

9% said that they were mostly heterosexual, 5% said they were in the middle, 7% said they were more homosexual than heterosexual, and 9% said they were homosexual. Thus 16% admitted that they were either homosexual or inclined in that direction, hardly the large number claimed by such "studies" as those of A. W. Richard Sipe or the *Kansas City Star*.

The second question (56) is "Which of the following statements most closely describes how you feel about the role that celibacy plays in your life?"

1. Celibacy is not a problem for me and I do not waver in my vows

2. Celibacy takes time to achieve and I consider it an ongoing journey

3. Celibacy is a discipline I try to follow, but do not always succeed

4. Celibacy is not relevant to my priesthood and I do not observe it

Thirty-three percent asserted that they do not waver and 50% that celibacy is an "ongoing journey." Fourteen percent admitted that they try and do not always succeed, and 3% claimed that it is irrelevant and they do not observe it. Thus 17% of priests admit that they are not always faithful to their promise of celibacy.

One can perhaps fault the exact wording of the questions. Arguably one would like greater precision and less poetry such as "an ongoing journey," yet the survey staff seems to have approached the issues with a sense of delicacy and restraint.

If one combines by cross tabulation questions 55 and 56,[6]

---

6. By dividing the first item after the first three responses and the second item between the second and third response.

one could conclude that 72% of American priests are hetero-sexual celibates, 10% are homosexual celibates, and 18% are not celibate, two-thirds of them heterosexuals and one-third homosexuals. If one considers only those who reject celibacy and remain priests, one discovers that they are 3.2% of the population of priests, half homosexual, half hetero-sexual.

Figure 1 illustrates the distribution of American priests by sexual orientation and behavior. The solid slice repre-sents heterosexual celibates. The horizontally lined slice still in the pie represents heterosexuals who have not al-ways been celibate. The two exploded slices represent ho-mosexual priests, the vertically lined slice homosexual celi-bates and the cross-hatched slice homosexuals who have not always been celibate.

The first question that arises concerning this distribu-tion is whether the sizable proportion of respondents who

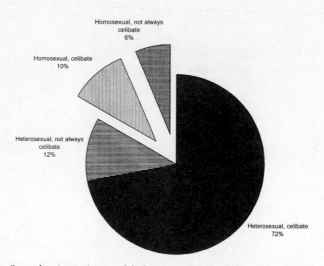

Fig. 1 Sexual orientation and behavior of priests. Data from Los Angeles Times Poll, 2002, questions 55 and 56.

admit that they are or have been sexually active and 16% who say that they are homosexual or mostly homosexual are shocking numbers. By the standards of the ideal of celibacy, any deviation is unacceptable. By the standards of the rumors, private and public, the numbers may seem less shocking. Only 4% of the respondents failed to answer each question, and only 7% rejected both items. Given the fact that opposition to the study in the Catholic press might have persuaded more conservative priests not to answer, one might tentatively judge that the proportions reported are close to the outer limits of the homosexual and sexually active proportions in the priesthood.

The second pertinent question is whether priests' age correlates with their sexual orientation and behavior. Table 1 addresses that question. Several conclusions seem to follow from a consideration of the table.

Homosexuals are present in every age group of priests, even among those over seventy-five, though in smaller proportions among the oldest and the youngest. Thus the argu-

Table 1 Age, Sexual Orientation, and Behavior of Priests, Percentage of Respondents

|  | 35 and Under | 36–45 | 46–55 | 56–65 | 66–75 | Over 75 | All |
|---|---|---|---|---|---|---|---|
| Heterosexual, celibate | 83 | 72 | 62 | 66 | 77 | 84 | 72 |
| Heterosexual, not always celibate | 8 | 7 | 10 | 12 | 14 | 12 | 12 |
| Homosexual, celibate | 7 | 18 | 17 | 12 | 5 | 2 | 10 |
| Homosexual, not always celibate | 3 | 3 | 11 | 10 | 4 | 2 | 6 |
| Celibacy irrelevant | (1) | (2) | (4) | (5) | (3) | (1) | (3) |
| N | 84 | 229 | 369 | 422 | 454 | 296 | 1,854 |

*Source:* Data from Los Angeles Times Poll, 2002, questions 55 and 56.
*Note:* Percentages in parentheses are a subset of respondents who are not always celibate.

ment that homosexuality is a new "challenge" for the priesthood does not seem to be valid.[7] On the other hand, the heaviest concentration of homosexuals is among the cohorts who were between thirty-six and sixty-five at the time of the study (2002), 28% of priests between forty-six and fifty-five and 22% of those between fifty-six and sixty-five. Eleven percent and 10%, respectively, of priests in these two groups are sexually active homosexuals in the sense that they admit that they sometimes fail in their struggle to be celibate.

The proportion of heterosexual priests who have not always been celibate is higher among those over forty-five, approximately one out of ten in each age cohort. The highest proportion (14%) is in the cohort between sixty-six and seventy-five.

The majority of homosexuals in every age group are celibate, though the proportion of heterosexuals who are celibate is much higher.

About a fifth of priests between forty-six and seventy-five admit that they have failed to live up to their celibacy promises. However, only a small proportion of priests dismiss celibacy as irrelevant to their ministry and assert they do not feel themselves bound by it. Thus one also concludes that most of those who have failed at celibacy say that they are trying.

Two-thirds of priests are celibate heterosexuals. Only those between thirty-six and forty-five fall below this proportion (to 62%).

The sexual behavior of those over seventy-five—14% have not always been celibate, most of them heterosexual—

---

7. There are no differences in sexual orientation or sexual behavior between diocesan priests and religious-order priests.

suggests that problems with sexuality are not new in the Church.

Table 1 may well be an inkblot: one can draw from it whatever conclusions one wants to make for or against celibacy. Much depends on the quality of life those in the various categories report, an issue to which we will turn in the next chapter.

When asked, most priests—three out of four—say that celibacy is no more difficult for homosexual priests than for heterosexuals. Nine out of ten homosexual priests deny that there is a difference, though the data would seem to suggest that there might be.

## HOMOSEXUAL SUBCULTURES

Cozzens (2000) has argued that distinctive homosexual subcultures are present both in seminaries and in dioceses, an assertion that apparently cost him his job as the rector of the Cleveland diocesan seminary. However, 45% of the priests in the 2002 survey agreed that such subcultures existed in their dioceses, and 28% agreed that they existed in the seminaries they had attended.

Table 2 indicates that more than two-fifths of priests between thirty-six and seventy-five who are not homosex-

Table 2 Homosexual Subcultures in Your Diocese and Seminary by Age, Percentage Who Answered Certainly or Probably

|  | 35 and Under | 36–45 | 46–55 | 56–65 | 66–75 | Over 75 | All |
|---|---|---|---|---|---|---|---|
| Diocese |  |  |  |  |  |  |  |
| Heterosexuals | 39 | 44 | 51 | 52 | 45 | 30 | 44 |
| Homosexuals | 25 | 47 | 56 | 53 | 63 | 54 | 53 |
| Seminary |  |  |  |  |  |  |  |
| Heterosexuals | 30 | 51 | 46 | 23 | 15 | 9 | 28 |
| Homosexuals | 50 | 43 | 48 | 24 | 20 | 9 | 35 |

*Source:* Data from Los Angeles Times Poll, 2002, questions 53 and 54.

ual believe that subcultures exist in their diocese, as do more than half of homosexual priests. Moreover, half of the homosexual priests fifty-five and under believe that there were such subcultures in their seminaries. Among heterosexual priests those who had observed such subcultures are concentrated between age thirty-six and fifty-five. One might read tables 1 and 2 and conclude that the ordination of homosexual priests and the formation of homosexual subcultures has perhaps diminished in recent years, possibly because of pressure on seminary rectors to deal with the "problem."

Why do homosexual men become priests in a proportion higher than their presence in the American population? Why have they apparently become more likely to choose the priesthood than they were in previous years? It is possible that older men did not have the thought categories to define homosexuality in the years before 1960. It does not seem likely that gay men become priests so that they will have easy access to gay sexual partners, because most of them are either celibate or trying to be celibate. Perhaps the priesthood is a profession in which a man without a wife does not have to explain why he is not married. However, the obvious subcultures suggest that homosexual priests are not interested in hiding their sexual orientation. It might be possible, as Cozzens (2000) seems to suggest, that gay men, even if they are celibate, need other gay men as close companions. It might be that the motives of homosexual men for choosing the priesthood are not greatly different from that of heterosexual men, a possibility that I will examine in the next chapter.

At this writing the Vatican is alleged to be considering a ban on the ordination of homosexuals, a prohibition that some might think is naïve about the history of the priesthood and indeed of the Vatican itself. Clearly there have been gay bishops, gay popes, and gay saints. Moreover, the Catholic Church has no monopoly, it would seem, on homosexual clerics.

Yet another question is whether it is appropriate that the priesthood be approximately 20% homosexual. Might the existence of homosexual subcultures frighten off young heterosexual men who are considering the priesthood? Or are young people today far more tolerant of homosexuals than are their elders? Might it be that homosexual men, despite what the Vatican calls their "objective disorder," bring to the priesthood some resources that it otherwise would not have?

These are questions of policy, taste, and ideology that the social scientist cannot answer. It must be noted, however, that most priests are heterosexual and that most homosexual priests appear to be celibate. Thus those who shrilly insist that it is time to say "goodbye to good men" are merely displaying their own homophobia.

One must also consider the possibility that a priesthood with a higher proportion of homosexuals might provide a haven for child abusers. While most homosexuals are not abusers and most abusers are not homosexuals, the propensity of Catholic conservatives to claim that child abuse is essentially a homosexual problem must be considered. However, those who argue in such fashion, no matter how exalted their positions in the Church might be, have yet to offer anything but their own unsubstantiated assertions to support their argument.

Since many abuses were committed by men who were ordained long before homosexuality became visible in the seminaries and the dioceses, the argument that there is a link between the increased presence of homosexuals and child abuse seems inherently improbable. However, this study is not about pedophiles but about the impact of child abuse on the priesthood. In a later chapter we will examine the reaction of priests, both heterosexual and homosexual, to child abuse. Homosexual priests are significantly more likely than heterosexual priests to think that it is the biggest crisis in the history of the Church in this country.

## INTIMACY

Both the 1970 NORC study and Nestor's 1993 dissertation gave Catholic priests high scores on measures of intimacy skills. No such personality scales were included in the 2002 *Times* study. However, question 58 asks about intimacy: "As you know, intimacy may be defined as a basic human need that includes close non-sexual bonds with personal friends. How satisfied are you with the level of that type of intimacy in your life?" Priests reported that they were either "very satisfied" (43%) or "mostly satisfied" (46%). Ninety-two percent of heterosexual priests were very or mostly satisfied as opposed to 80% of the homosexual priests. While those who are youngest and oldest have the highest score on "very satisfied" (51% and 60% respectively) the lowest scores are for those between forty-five and sixty-five—only about 30% say they are "very satisfied" with their intimate relationships.

Perhaps homosexual priests are not satisfied because they perceive barriers to relationships with both priests and laity. Yet intimacy satisfaction goes down for both homosexual and heterosexual priests between forty-five and sixty-five. Perhaps those years are the winter of discontent for priests—or merely midlife crises. These issues will be examined in greater detail in chapter 3. Note that the large proportion of priests who claim intimate relationships is consistent with Nestor's observations.

## SUMMARY

Data show that most priests are both heterosexual and celibate. There is a higher proportion of homosexual priests among those in the middle years of life. The majority of them, however, are celibate or at least try to be. Those who disregard the celibacy rule completely are a tiny fraction of priests, no more than 3%. The perception is widespread that there are homosexual subcultures in both dioceses and seminaries. Most priests are satisfied with the quality of intimacy in their lives, straights more than gays, younger and older men more than men in the middle years of life.

# 3

## THE MORALE QUESTION

G ranted, at least for the sake of argument, that most priests are celibate heterosexuals and that most of the others at least strive for celibacy, what impact does this kind of life have on the happiness of those who practice celibacy or at least attempt to practice it? Let us also grant, again for the sake of argument, that the personality tests administered by NORC in 1970 and by Nestor in 1993 suggest that these men are not without some capacity for intimacy, is it possible that they sublimate the basic human propensities for sexual union and for parenthood without paying a heavy emotional price? While their dedication is perhaps admirable, can such a constrained and restrained existence permit much happiness?

Doubtless there are those who deny the premises behind this question. Despite the personality tests, priests must be emotional wrecks, their human nature twisted and drained of basic human emotions. Thus a woman writing in the Jesuit magazine *America* says, "Sensible people judge the practice by its fruits, its efficacy. The many troubles that celibates have displayed in recent years have given lie to the argument that abstinence is something intrinsically superior to sexual experience." The logic of this argument is that the "troubles that celibates have displayed" make celibacy an intrinsically inferior way of life. Apparently, the many troubles married laymen have had are irrelevant to the discussion. Anyone who thinks that marriage or sexual relations solve many male (or female) problems has not paid much attention to the human condition.

The issue in this book is not whether celibacy is superior or not, but whether it creates major psychological problems for those in the Catholic priesthood who practice it. To a considerable extent this discussion is pointless, since everyone knows that priests are an emotional mess. Nonetheless, one who believes in scholarship must present the evidence.

Several studies suggest that, oddly perhaps, most priests like being priests and are happy in their lives and work, despite the absence of sexual relationships and family life. To put it another way, celibate priests on the average, far from being wretchedly unhappy men, are very happy indeed. In some circumstances, then, celibacy is not a barrier to human happiness.

It does not follow, I hasten to add, that the celibacy rule is part of the essence of the Catholic Church, much less that it cannot or should not be changed. Arguably it ought to be changed. The point here is that among the valid reasons for change is not that priests are unhappy and frustrated men. On the basis of all the evidence available to us, that is simply not the truth, no matter how many observers are persuaded that it is.

Fortunately for the purposes of this analysis two items from the 1970 NORC study are repeated in the two *Times* surveys (15 and 18 in the 2002 study)—whether the respondent would choose to be a priest again and whether he will leave the priesthood. In the 1970 NORC study seven out of eight priests said they would certainly or probably choose to be priests again (table 3). Thirty years later, in the *Times* survey, that proportion rose to nine out of ten, higher than the proportion of married people who said they would choose the same spouse again. Seven out of ten said cer-

Table 3 Priest Morale at Three Times, Percentage of Respondents

| | 1970 | 1993 | 2002 |
|---|---|---|---|
| Would choose priesthood again | 78 | 90 | 92 |
| Satisfied as priest | | 89 | 93 |
| Turned out better[a] | | 56 (31) | 63 (29) |
| Will not leave | 87 | 87 | 89 |
| Advise young man to enter | | | 91 |

Sources: Data from NORC study, 1970; Los Angeles Times Poll, 1993; Los Angeles Times Poll, 2002, questions 13–18.

[a] The first number is for the response "better than expected." The number in parentheses is for "about as expected."

tainly to both of these items, 20% more said probably. Moreover, at all three times approximately seven out of eight priests said they would certainly not leave the priesthood, and only 2% said they would certainly leave.

In the *Times* studies (question 13) approximately nine out of ten respondents said that they were either very or somewhat (20%) satisfied with their life as a priest. And when asked how their priestly life had turned out (14), 63% said in 2002 it was better than they had expected, and 29% more said that it was as good as they had expected. In 2002 the favorable proportions, already at a high level of approval, had all risen a few percentage points. Either priests in 2002 did not realize that they were under pressure or did not let it interfere with their happiness. Nine out of ten also said they would advise a young man who seemed qualified that perhaps he should pursue a priestly vocation (which is not quite the same as actively recruiting him).

How do Catholic priests compare with Protestant clergy in their job and life satisfaction? In 2001, under a commission from the Pulpit and Pew center at Duke Divinity School, NORC interviewed 883 pastors from a random sample of the American population, of whom 189 were Catholic priests (Carroll 2002). The response rate was 73%. Surprisingly the priests scored highest on most indicators: 76% of priests, 61% of Mainline Protestant ministers, and

73% of Conservative Protestant ministers said that they had never thought of leaving the active ministry. (Two percent of the priests said that they thought very often of leaving, the same proportion as in the 2002 *Times* study.[1]) Eighty-six percent of the priests and approximately 70% of the ministers said they were very satisfied with their current job. Fifty-seven percent of the priests and 38% of the ministers were very satisfied with the quality of their spiritual life. Eighty-eight percent of the priests and 71% of the ministers said that they were very satisfied with their lay leaders. Thus, as far as these indicators of morale are concerned, celibacy does not seem to be an obstacle to the job satisfaction and spiritual satisfaction of the Catholic clergy.

Thirteen percent of the Mainline Protestants and 73% of the Conservatives were satisfied with their family life, as compared with 75% of all Americans. Moreover, the strongest negative correlation with general satisfaction among clergy was −.23 with spouse's resentment of financial situation.

Yet an article in the Protestant journal the *Christian Century* (Jones 2002) reported that news of the Pulpit and Pew study was so different "from the dominant religious story and scandal and cover up in the Roman Catholic Church." The *Christian Century* failed to note the higher morale among priests than among Protestant clergy.

It is useful also to compare the satisfaction of priests with that of other professions. In 2001 half of physicians said that they would not recommend "the practice of medicine as a profession to a young person today" (Kaiser Family Foundation 2002). In 2000 75% of the young lawyers in the country said that they were satisfied with the "practice

1. The similarity of morale responses between the 2002 *Times* study and the Pulpit and Pew study suggests that, despite its lower response rate, the *Times* study is broadly reflective of the situation in the priesthood.

of law" (27% "very satisfied"; 48% "somewhat satisfied"; $N = 787$; American Bar Association 2001). A 1999 study carried out by my NORC colleague Allen Sanderson reported that 63% of college faculty said they would certainly become faculty again, and 24% probably (Sanderson 2000).

Thus willingness to choose the same career again or satisfaction with the choice is higher for priests than for doctors, lawyers, and faculty members. Their satisfaction is in general higher than that of Protestant clergy (whose estimate of the quality of their family life ought to be chilling to priests who so readily believe that pastoring and family can be easily reconciled).

Men enjoy being priests. Unfortunately that is not the public image that they have permitted others to create for them.

Table 4 shows that heterosexuals overwhelmingly indicate that they would choose the priesthood again and that it has been better than they thought it would be. Homosexuals are less enthusiastic. But except for those between forty-six and fifty-five, the majority are firmly committed to their priestly vocation.

Why are the scores somewhat lower for gay priests? Perhaps because a homosexual's life can be difficult even out-

Table 4 Satisfaction in the Priesthood by Age and Sexual Orientation, Percentage of Respondents

|  | 35 and Under | 36–45 | 46–55 | 56–65 | 66–75 | Over 75 | All |
|---|---|---|---|---|---|---|---|
| Certainly choose again |  |  |  |  |  |  |  |
| Heterosexual | 78 | 81 | 72 | 67 | 77 | 85 | 76 |
| Homosexual | 63 | 50 | 48 | 52 | 69 | 63 | 53 |
| Better than expected |  |  |  |  |  |  |  |
| Heterosexual | 68 | 66 | 62 | 64 | 70 | 66 | 74 |
| Homosexual | 50 | 37 | 44 | 52 | 63 | 73 | 53 |

Source: Data from Los Angeles Times Poll, 2002, questions 14 and 15.

side the priesthood and that homosexuals experience more pressures inside it than do straight priests.

Finally 45% of the priests who admit that they have been sexually active say they would certainly choose the priesthood again, and 30% more say they probably would, while 50% of the group say the priesthood has been better than they expected and another 33% say that it is about what they expected.

There are two proper responses with which the social scientist should greet these data. The first is surprise, not to say astonishment. The second is to wonder how the priesthood, for all its problems, its failings, its imperfections, can have such an enormous appeal to those who are part of it. It will simply not do to proclaim that they are not telling the truth or that they are suppressing their subconscious feelings. Nor is it appropriate, for someone who claims to be a scholar, simply to dismiss or ignore these findings.

## SOURCES OF CHALLENGE
## AND SATISFACTION

Two open-ended questions (11 and 12) in the *Times* survey give us some hints about why morale is so high among priests.

> What are the greatest joys that you receive in your life and work as a priest today?
>
> What are the greatest challenges you face in your life and work as a priest today?

Five answers were recorded for each question. I chose to analyze the first response because it represented the respondent's spontaneous initial response. The *Times* coded thirty answers to the first question, and I recoded them to nine—helping others (17%), saying Mass (13%), administering the sacraments (13%), strengthening the faith of the laity (9%), doing God's work (7%), sharing your life with others (7%), preaching (6%), teaching (2%), and others (27%). While "helping others" is the largest spontaneous response and one that is not necessarily unreligious, most of the other responses are explicitly religious—saying Mass, administering the sacraments, preaching, doing God's work. Priests are altruists perhaps, but for the most part their altruism is religiously oriented—the altar, the font, and the pulpit. These activities bring joy to the lives of priests and apparently sustain them in their work. One may combine these categories into two—the sacred and the profane. The former combine the formally religious—Mass, sacraments, preaching, doing God's work, and building the faith of the laity. The latter are more generally altruistic—helping others and sharing in their lives. About half of the priests gave a "sacred" answer and another quarter a "profane" one—though helping others can be at least implicitly religious activity. The response pattern for homosexual priests is somewhat different because they are four percentage points less likely than heterosexual priests to mention the Mass as a source of joy, and three percentage points more likely to mention preaching. However, it is impossible to escape the conclusion that gay priests enjoy the priesthood for similar reasons as do straight priests. Finally the response pattern does not vary much across age categories: approximately half the priests emphasize the explicitly religious aspects of their ministry and another quarter emphasize the altruistic (while the final quarter is distributed among other lesser sources of joy). There are, as we shall see later, substantial intergenerational differences among priests, but they do not disagree about the sources of joy in their lives. Priests like to be priests because they like doing the things that priests do. The 1970 NORC study reports similar findings: four out of five priests report great satisfaction from saying Mass and administering the sacraments.

This is a fact that the secular reader might find difficult to understand. How can men give up the pleasures of the bedroom and the hearth for such insubstantial realities as serving God, administering the sacraments, preaching, and saying Mass (or presiding over the Eucharist, to use the liturgically correct words)? No attempt to make this choice seem rational to the secular reader could possibly succeed. Such a reader cannot dismiss priests as unbalanced or immature, however, because the personality scales already cited establish that, on average, they are not.

The late Cardinal Emanuel Suhard of Paris once remarked that bearing witness does not mean to engage in propaganda but to live one's life in a way that would be foolish if Jesus were not the son of God. Willy-nilly, the priest is a sign of the transcendent, even if it turns out that there is no transcendent. He has bet his life on Pascal's wager, found it better than he had expected, and on balance would make the same wager again. In the current climate of anti-Catholicism, he still seems mad. That may be why anti-Catholics through the whole history of the United States have railed against celibacy.

Celibacy is not part of the essence of the priesthood, as the practices of the Greek churches (both Catholic and Orthodox) make clear. Perhaps the celibacy rule ought to be repealed. Perhaps it is essential that it be repealed if the Catholic laity are to have enough priests. Perhaps there would be as much satisfaction in the priestly life if priests had wives and children. Perhaps if priests could marry, young men would flock to the priesthood. Or perhaps not. Social science cannot presently answer those questions. It can say, however, that something about the priest is remarkable, and it is not unhealthy by our current measures of personal and professional happiness and psychological well-being.

The *Times* survey unit divided the responses to the challenges question into fifty-four categories. Many responses were essentially complaints about the world—the media, the lack of faith, secularism, materialism, individualism, apathy, indifference, ignorance, passivity, problematic parishioners. Almost a quarter of the priests listed these as the most serious challenges they had to face. Less than 2% named celibacy. Six percent were concerned about the sexual abuse crisis. Eight percent listed health problems and 24% other personal problems—workload, burnout, meeting people's expectations, no time for prayer or spiritual life, lack of perseverance, loneliness, excessive administrative demands, and personal financial issues. Eleven percent were concerned about direct problems of the ministry— effective ministry, helping others, keeping the Church and the Gospel relevant, evangelization, helping the poor and the impoverished, granting more power to the laity.

Homosexual priests are notably less likely (12% versus 26%) to indulge in the listing of such cosmic challenges, but not because they are more worried about ministerial problems. Rather they are more likely to find loneliness and the need for privacy as challenges in their lives.

The laity might perhaps take offense that so few of the priests' perceived challenges focused on their ministerial activities and so many on denunciation of the world or personal concerns. They also might wonder why, given the magnitude of the sexual abuse problem and the fury of the laity, no more than 6% of priests felt challenged by it.

These issues adumbrate a problem to which we return in subsequent chapters. Priests are personally satisfied and reasonably mature, despite celibacy, but they seem curiously out of touch with the laity, the world in which the laity live, and the religious problems the laity have. It may be all well and good to rail against the media, the lack of faith, secularism, materialism, individualism, apathy, indifference, ignorance, passivity, and such problems (as the curial cardinals do when discussing the United States). One may gain a good deal of satisfaction from such complaints, but they are so general and so abstract that it is not clear what such denunciations accomplish. Why do not more priests, the clients might well wonder, find challenge in ministerial concerns? Why does not a single respondent report that he finds challenge in preparing and delivering sermons? How much denial is required for a priest not to find sermons a serious challenge?

To make matters worse, the very youngest priests (35 and under) are the most likely (30%) to have given themselves over to weltschmerz, a curious pessimism in those who haven't had many years in the priesthood. (Only a fifth of those over seventy-five feel the same way.) The young are also twice as likely as older priests to think that sexual abuse is a serious problem.

Some seminary faculty say that young priests, some of the so-called belated vocations, have come to the priesthood as a way of escaping from the evils of the world. The data reported here are not incompatible with such an assertion. The difficulty with such an approach is that it pretty much neglects the Catholic laity, save as targets for denunciation.

As I was working on this chapter, a young woman remarked to me with considerable astonishment that her pastor repeatedly complained to the parish that no one would come to evening meetings. He can't understand, she said, what evening is like in two-career families with small children. Such a lack of understanding presumably would not occur if there were a married clergy. Or if more priests had even a slight touch of sensitivity.

## JOY AND MORALE

There are substantial and statistically significant positive correlations between "sacred" joys and morale in the priesthood. Those who mentioned such joys were approximately ten percentage points more likely to say that the priesthood is better than expected, that they would choose to be priests again, that they are very satisfied with their priesthood, and that they will certainly not leave. There are also negative correlations between "profane" joys and these morale measures, though the majority were still more than satisfied. The priesthood then seems to be less a profession for pure altruists than for religious altruists.

There are also statistically significant positive correlations with the morale measures for those who report that their challenges are from ministry concerns. Those priests who have the highest morale are those who find joy in the sacred dimension of their work and in the ministerial challenges they face. Unfortunately they are only 7% of the sample, but 99% of them say they would certainly or probably choose to be a priest again as opposed to 88% whose joys are more profane and who complain about the world. Eighty percent of the former say they are very satisfied with the priesthood, compared to 63% of the latter.

## SUMMARY

Priests are clearly happy and satisfied men. They report on the average that the priesthood has been better than they had expected it would be, that they are very satisfied with their lives as priests, that they would choose to be a priest again, and that they are not likely to leave the priesthood. They score higher on measures of satisfaction than do doctors, lawyers, faculty members, and Protestant ministers. There are differences between homosexual priests and heterosexual priests on these measures, though the majority of gay priests score positively on indicators of satisfaction. Moreover, regardless of their age, priests are most likely to find joys in their priesthood from explicitly religious work, whatever their age and their sexual orientation.

There are some interesting differences, however, across age lines in the descriptions of "greatest challenges" in the priesthood. The youngest clergy are more likely to see challenge in a world that they view negatively and in their response to the sexual abuse scandal, perhaps because they became priests to escape from an environment that they find evil. The highest scores on the morale measures are among that small group who find joy in sacred work and challenge in ministerial demands.

It is clear that homosexual priests in general find the same challenges in the priesthood and the same joys, though they are more likely to say they find joy in preaching. Differences in sexual orientation may be extremely important in the human condition, but they do not seem to make much difference in the satisfaction men find in being a priest.

Despite the good news about priestly morale, there is a shadow of bad news in the fact that priests do not seem to be in tune with their lay folk, especially on the need for better ministry and for a response to the sexual abuse crisis. Not one of them mentioned the challenge of better preaching.

# 4

## WHY THEY LEAVE

"During the research we heard numerous stories of priests who fell in love and the ones who subsequently resigned usually had felt dissatisfaction with the priesthood before they entered into the love relationship. Happy and fulfilled priests rarely resign even if they are in love" (Hoge 2002). There are two reasons why Dean Hoge's comment is important. He is not a priest, nor even a Catholic. And he works usually with the support of the National Federation of Priests' Councils, an organization of priests that has consistently argued that men leave the priesthood because of celibacy. The NFPC has consistently written off my work since their first president demanded the data from the 1970 NORC study and then commissioned a study to counteract it. It has never quite forgiven me for my argument in the study that men tend to leave the priesthood because they are not happy in their work and that the desire to marry comes from that unhappiness. Indeed. The leadership of the NFPC is quite capable intellectually of insisting that Hoge is right and I'm wrong, though we're saying the same thing.

We have already learned that priests are not immature and are capable of intimacy as measured by Shostrom's POI and the scales Nestor used, that most of them are celibate heterosexuals, and that they are happy in the priesthood, despite clerical celibacy—a picture exactly the opposite of that offered by Eugene Cullen Kennedy and A. W. Richard

Sipe.[1] In this chapter I address the question of whether celibacy drives men out of the priesthood. The answer is that about a sixth of the men who leave do so primarily because of celibacy.

Many of those who have left the active priesthood in the last thirty years have named celibacy as their reason for leaving and insist that they would return to the active ministry if they could do so as a married man. Many Catholic liberals have argued that if married priests were admitted back into the active ministry they would go a long way toward easing the shortage of priests.

Doubtless some of them would, and I have no quarrel with their good faith. However, in the NORC project (1972) we also surveyed a sample of resigned priests. Forty percent agreed that they would return to the priesthood if they could, but only half of that 40% said they would be willing to go back to the work they had been doing, either parish work or teaching. Thus about a fifth of the resigned priests actually liked the work they were doing. Since much of the satisfaction of being a priest comes from the work, it should be clear that four out of five who left did not like the work they had been doing. If one is unhappy in the priesthood, one is very likely to fall in love. Indeed, it might be argued that if one is unhappy, one should fall in love.

Celibacy in general becomes a problem only when one is not obtaining satisfactions from work. Men should be able to leave the priesthood with the Church's gratitude and honor when they feel they can no longer stand it. How-

---

1. As I reread this chapter I am aware that it was written with some passion. It is not my intent to defend my own celibacy (as some critics will doubtlessly assert) but simply to defend the truth. Despite the talking heads, the conventional wisdom, the drumbeat of anticelibacy propaganda from national priest organizations and some former priests, most priests remain celibates and happy and are not willing to give up their priesthood or their celibacy.

ever, the argument that celibacy drove most of them out did not stand the test of the data in 1970 and still doesn't.[2]

The 1993 *Times* study asked questions that make it possible to reanalyze the issue, questions about whether a man would choose to be a priest again, about whether he would marry if the church permitted priestly marriage, and whether he might leave the priesthood. Sixteen percent of the priests in the 1993 *Times* study said they would certainly or probably marry if the Church permitted them to do so. When first confronted with that statistic, many dismiss it by saying, well yes, of course, those are the ones still in the priesthood, but look at those who have left. One of the implicit rules about the discussion of celibacy in progressive Catholic circles during the last couple of decades has been that the rare celibate who attempts to defend it is to be dismissed as self-justifying and self-serving, while the former priest (or former seminarian) who attacks it is never to be accused of trying to justify his own decisions.

In fact, most priests have not left the priesthood. Richard Schoenherr, the acknowledged expert in this area, estimated the resignation rate at 20% in 1984 and suggested that the average ordination-class resignation rate will reach just under 25% by the silver jubilee of the class. This is a substantial loss, but 75% will not have resigned, and the rate is somewhat lower than the divorce rate for married Catholics.

Neither the divorce rate of married men and women nor the defection rate of priests necessarily says anything about the happiness of those who do not leave the pool of matrimony or priesthood. The "rate" fallacy, so beloved by the

2. Nonetheless, in principle I would not be opposed to permitting some of them to return (perhaps on occasion) to exercising a priestly role.

popular media, is a misleading logical fallacy. The number in the numerator of a rate tells nothing about those who are in the denominator but not in the numerator. It may be that an increasing divorce rate indicates that the level of unhappiness in marriage is going up. But it is also possible that it indicates only that those who are unhappy in marriage are now more likely to leave than they used to be (especially women, because they have better control of their fertility and their financial situation).

Empirical investigation can show whether those who remain in the pool are less happy than they might have been before divorce became easier. By itself a rate indicates nothing. It may be that even those who do not leave a given pool are less happy than they used to be. Or it may be that those who leave do so because it is easier to leave than it used to be and that those who stay do so despite the availability of exit and continue to be as satisfied as they ever were.

I have established in my book *Faithful Attraction* that those who stay in marriages when it is relatively easy to leave do so because they enjoy their marriages and are relatively happy in them and hence have no desire or reason to leave. The divorce rate, it would appear, is rising because it is easier to get out of an unhappy marriage and not because the general level of marital happiness is declining. On the basis of the recent studies of the priesthood, the same is true of priests.

What, then, about the conventional wisdom? It can be articulated, I think, in the following propositions: (1) Those who leave the priesthood leave because they want to marry. Therefore, most priests want to marry. (2) Some of those who leave the priesthood are bitterly angry at the celibacy requirement and attack the Church for imposing it on them. Therefore, all priests resent the requirement. (3) If those who left to marry had been permitted to stay in the priesthood as married men, they would have stayed. (4) A proof of the problems of enforced celibacy are all the sexual abuse cases among priests.

Let me dispose of the last argument first. It is well known that sexual abuse is a syndrome acquired early in life and has nothing to do with celibacy. Most pedophiles are married men. Does it follow that marriage should be abolished because of that? Moreover, the problem is not limited to one denomination or one profession but affects all denominations (including those with a married clergy) and all professions that have access to children. Many married men are guilty of verbally, physically, or sexually abusing their wives and children. Does it follow that these are "fruits" of marriage and that marriage is therefore wrong?

The first proposition represents the "rate" fallacy in its most obvious form and would be on its face an absurd argument even if the data from the NORC study and the *Times* studies under consideration did not refute it. A parallel assertion about marriage would be that because many women who leave their husbands have been abused, most of those who have not left their husbands also have been abused.

Which comes first, dissatisfaction with the priesthood or the desire to marry? To put it more precisely, would those who want to marry (would marry if the Church permitted it) and are unhappy in the priesthood be more likely to leave than those who want to marry and are happy in the priesthood? If there is no difference or very little difference between the two groups, then it is celibacy as such that is driving men out of the priesthood. If, on the other hand, those in the first group are notably more likely to plan to leave than those in the second group, it is not celibacy by itself that is driving most men out of the priesthood, but unhappiness with the priesthood.

Almost half (48% in the 2002 *Times* study) of those who would marry if they could and who do not like the priesthood (who say they would not choose to be a priest again) are thinking of leaving the priesthood. However, only 7% of those who like the priesthood (who say they would be a priest again) and would marry if they could are thinking of leaving.

Thus it is not merely the desire to marry that causes most men to want to leave, but the desire to marry plus such intense dissatisfaction with the priesthood that they would not be a priest again. Moreover, even among those who would not marry if they could, 22% of those who are unhappy are thinking of leaving, as opposed to only 1% of those who are happy. Thus to produce high levels of resignation there must be a combination of dissatisfaction and a desire to marry. If only one is present, dissatisfaction is a higher predictor of the propensity to leave than a desire to marry.

To consider the matter another way (fig. 2), 68% of those who are thinking of leaving the priesthood would not choose to be a priest again, while 32% would choose to be a priest again. Only 16% of those thinking of leaving are satisfied with their priestly decision but want to marry. In figure 2, which is composed of all the men who were thinking they might leave the priesthood, the plain slice of the pie is those who regret their decision to become a priest and would marry if the Church permitted it. The slice with horizontal lines is those who regret their decision to become a priest yet would not marry, even if the Church permitted it. Finally the crosshatched slice is made up of those who are glad that they became priests but want to marry—

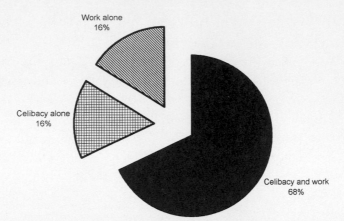

Fig. 2. Reasons for thinking of leaving the priesthood. Data from Los Angeles Times Poll, 1993, questions.

the ones who might be driven out of the priesthood by celibacy alone. Hence about one out of six are thinking about leaving a role that they would like except that they cannot marry.

That proportion (one out of six likely to leave the priesthood simply because of celibacy) is remarkably consistent with the estimate of one out of five in the 1970 NORC study, thirty years ago. Schoenherr estimated that 6,938 priests left between 1966 and 1984 (after which resignations declined). If one applies the 16% estimate from the present research retroactively, approximately 1,100 men left the priesthood only or mainly because of celibacy, and approximately 4,700 would not have chosen to be priests again, presumably because they did not like the work.

These are extrapolations, of course, but they are about the same numbers one would have predicted from the one-fifth who would have been willing to return as married men to ordinary priestly work, as measured in the NORC report.

One would like to know something more about the experience of priesthood by those 208 respondents who would like to marry but also like being priests and of the experience of celibacy by those 1,423 priests who like being priests and would not marry even if they could. There are no data that enable us to understand either sociologically or theologically the motives behind the astonishing statistics reported in this chapter. In an allegedly permissive society, what explains this commitment to celibacy?

I have heard it muttered that those who do not want to marry even if they are free to do so are either gay or neuter. We know from the 2002 study that most priests are not gay. But even if, for the sake of argument, we credit this explanation, it does not explain why more than two out of three priests who would marry if they could nonetheless choose not to leave the priesthood. Until we hear from them, we do not understand what it is about the priesthood that they like so much.

In fact 17% of those who were priests in 1993 would either certainly (5%) or probably (12%) marry if the Church gave permission for married priests: 3% of those over seventy-five; 8% of those between sixty-six and seventy-five; 15% (4% "certainly") of those between fifty-six and sixty-five; 24% (6% "certainly") of those between thirty-six and fifty-five; and 29% (8% "certainly") of those thirty-five and under. While most priests want celibacy made optional, they do not seem ready to exercise that option for themselves.

While I doubt that the logic of this statistical argument will change many minds, it does enable me to deny flatly that it is celibacy as such that has driven or still drives most men out of the priesthood. Confirming this argument is the fact that the present defection rates for married Protestant clergy, discussed in chapter 3, are higher than the present defection rates for priests. The strongest predictor of a Protestant cleric's decision to leave the ministry for a secular occupation is dissatisfaction with the work he has been doing. The pattern for leaving the ministry is ecumenical.

Dean Hoge again (2002): "Whether a priest is heterosexual or sexual, in love or not, it will not drive him to resign unless at the same time he feels lonely or unappreciated. This is the basic finding of our research." This dictum is confirmed by data in the 2002 *Times* study. Of those who said loneliness was one of their challenges, 57% say they will certainly not leave the priesthood as opposed to 81% who do not list loneliness as a challenge. Fortunately for the priesthood, only 2.3% said that loneliness was their major challenge.

That finding in itself is counterintuitive. Priests are supposed to be lonely. Aren't they lonely in most of the novels about priests?[3]

To argue as I do that celibate priests are neither emotionally immature nor unhappy and that most of them do not find celibacy an intolerable burden is not to make a case against the abolition of the celibacy rule. Celibacy is not the main reason why men leave, but it may be the main reason that men don't become priests. That is generally assumed to be the case, which is probably why the majority of priests support optional celibacy, though they themselves do not seem inclined to accept the option. (We shall return to the question of recruitment to the priesthood in a subsequent chapter.) Surely this assumption is supported by the fact of the sexual revolution, a fact that, as we have seen earlier, needs careful definition. Yet it has also been assumed that celibacy is the main reason that men leave the priesthood, and as I have shown, that seems problematic at best. It is difficult to see how the sexual revolution de-

---

3. In my own novels, Blackie Ryan is anything but lonely, perhaps because, like the author who created him and like most priests, he is too busy to be lonely.

scribed earlier is going to increase a young man's desire to make love to a woman or to be joined with a woman in a permanent union, at least not without a major change in the evolutionary process that suddenly makes young women more attractive to young men than they were 40 years ago, or 400 years ago, for that matter. It is absurd, almost funny, to suggest that there is more sexual fantasy, more sexual drive, more obscene thoughts, more sexual energy, more sexual hunger, more desire for a wife and children of one's own than there were, let us say, in 1944 or 944. Have testosterone levels in the youthful male increased in the last half century? Has the increase of nudity in films and on television notably heightened male sexual need? Have loneliness and fear of loneliness increased since 1944? Have dreams of marital bliss grown more appealing since then? Has the appeal of intimate companionship with a member of the opposite sex as a temporary escape from mortality grown more powerful?

In a certain sense the findings of this chapter heighten the mystery of priestly celibacy. Priests, the data seem to show us, are emotionally mature men (in comparison with other men) who are happy in their work. Moreover, celibacy has not driven most of them out of the priesthood. Now we learn that the majority would remain celibate even if they were free to marry. How can this be?

That question will not be important for those who deny any or all of the links in the chain of argument around which this book is built. However, the question is important for two groups of readers—priests themselves and secularists who are willing to accept the chain of argument as a working hypothesis.

It is not an easy question to answer, in great part because little attention has been paid to the theological, sociological, and psychological issues of celibate sublimation. Since

it is generally assumed that celibacy is unhealthy sexual repression, it has seemed unnecessary to try to understand
it. Yet if most priests are, as the data suggest, neither unhealthy nor repressed, then they are a mystery that demands a more careful examination by serious scholars.

Would not married priests be able to perform the same
religious and altruistic functions that celibate priests do?
Why then would so many priests be willing to cling to their
celibacy even if they were free to relinquish it? One can
offer only hypotheses to be tested in the unlikely event that
more serious research might be undertaken on the positive
functions of celibacy.

Perhaps priests sense that much of what they do would
not be possible if they had a wife and family. The married
clergymen of other denominations claim that they are just
as diligent in their work as priests and that in fact their
spouse makes it possible for them to be even more diligent.
Most priests are willing to accept that argument because
they don't want to offend anyone these days. Yet the hours
in the day are not infinitely expandable. Perhaps celibacy
is valuable to priests precisely because it gives them more
time to engage in work that they find inherently satisfying.

Perhaps after a few years in the ministry, priests slip
into the comfortable position of an incorrigible bachelor,
content with a situation in which neither wife nor children
violate their peace and privacy, secure from the invasion
of one's private life by those who are different.

Perhaps they come to understand that they have formed
long-term habits and priorities that would have to be given
up should they decide to share their lives with a woman.

Perhaps after a certain number of years they have come
to understand that marriage is not an easy relationship, despite its obvious rewards. It imposes serious demands on

the marriage partners, demands that cannot always be ne-
gotiated without conflict, sometimes very serious conflict.

Perhaps they value the nongenital intimate relationships
they have with so many people too much to give them up.
Consider again part of the earlier quote from Nestor (1993):
"Priests demonstrated more eagerness to enter into relationships of varying depths and they reported that they enjoy providing support, nurturance, care, and concern to
others more than other men did."

Perhaps the challenges of courting and bedding a
woman, and sharing with her the same house as well as
bedroom, never easy for any man at any age in life, are too
overwhelming.

These tentative probes I hesitantly throw out into the
dark. Some day someone will do a study in which they ask
priests what they get out of celibacy and why they would
be reluctant to give it up. Then we will begin to have a
rational choice model to account for celibacy. However, unless priests are madmen—and patently they are not—there
must be reasons to choose their celibate commitment and
not merely as an investment in a Pascalian payoff in the
world to come.

Research my colleagues and I did on young Catholics
(Greeley et al. 1981) points in a direction worth exploring,
perhaps because it fits some of my experiences and is com-
patible with the Nestor quote. Young men whose wife had
a "confidante" relationship with a priest were more likely
than others to support the continuation of clerical celibacy,
but they were also more likely to support the ordination of
women, suggesting that they could see the advantage of a
cross-gender confidante relationship in their own lives. On
a more general level Catholic men and women are (or perhaps were) willing to share an enormous amount of their

confidences with a priest, even a young one with the oils of ordination scarcely dry on his hands. These confidences are an almost daily event in the lives of many priests, events that perhaps they sense they would have to give up if they had a wife.[4]

4. And it makes for much more poignant stories. If I am correct that stories keep Catholics in their religion despite the imbecilities of their leadership, maybe it's the stories that keep men in the celibate priesthood.

# 5

## PRIESTS AND THE CATHOLIC REVOLUTION

The Catholic Church experienced two traumatic events in the second half of the twentieth century: the reforms of the Second Vatican Council between 1962 and 1965, initiated by Pope John in resistance to those he called the prophets of doom, and the subsequent attempts of the prophets of doom to restore the status quo ante after the Council adjourned, attempts in which many of the leaders of the Council engaged because they were frightened by the apparent demons that the very mild council reforms had unleashed. Both events have had a profound effect on the Catholic priesthood all over the world.

Melissa Wilde (2002) has observed that the bishops, excited by the discovery that they now had the power to change the Church despite the Roman curia, were swept up in what sociologist Émile Durkheim called "effervescence," and by a sense that the Holy Spirit was guiding them.[2] They had no intention of destabilizing the structures (patterns of behavior and the motivations that support them; Sewell 1996) of the Catholic Church. However, even modest changes contradicted the belief that the Catholic Church had not changed, would not change, and could not change, which had underpinned the structures of the church's re-

---

1. The Church must always be reformed.
2. Whether She was or not the sociologist cannot say.

sponse to the French Revolution. For the lower clergy and the laity, the changes and the effervescence that accompanied them, reported by the media of the world, were an exciting and exhilarating series of events, the most important religious events of their lives for many of them.

## THE CATHOLIC REVOLUTION

The lower clergy and the laity engaged in a revolution (Sewell 1996) in the late 1960s and early 1970s in which they decided that, since the Church was changing, there were some changes they could opt for while the Church was catching up (Greeley 2003). No doctrines were repealed. Everyone continued to believe in God, Jesus, Church, Mary, Pope. But the credibility of the Church's sexual ethic was devastated. The laity, with the support of the lower clergy, concluded that they would no longer give the hierarchy the right to control their sex lives. The reform of the Council had slipped out of the control of the hierarchy. The leadership of the Church has tried to regain control by renewed repression, especially with the birth-control encyclical in 1968, four years after the end of the Council. This was, as any social science adviser might have told them, the worst possible response to the fluid situation. In a crisis one is not likely to do wise and sophisticated things but to do the things that one does well—in this case, make rules, lay down laws, and issue orders. Authority must impose its will on the laity, not listen to them. As a result the evidence shows beyond doubt that the laity and lower clergy simply turned the leadership off.

As we shall see, however, the leadership has begun to produce a clergy that would like to rebuild the Church that it perceives existed before the Council—thus introducing a cleavage between the middle-aged clergy and the younger. The present situation has soured the hopes of many of those who lived through the excitement and the promise of the Council and now must accept both the shattering of their dreams and the appearance of younger clergy for whom the Council never happened.

## IS THE REFORM IMPULSE STILL ALIVE?

Hence the question arises as to whether the spirit of reform still exists in the priesthood, especially on moral matters of sex and gender and institutional matters of priesthood. The 1970 NORC study asked questions about birth control, premarital sex, abortion, and masturbation. It also asked questions about attitudes five years before on premarital sex and birth control (table 5). With the two *Times* studies, we thus have information across thirty-eight years.

The sex and gender issues of reform are part of the Catholic revolution, the laity and the lower clergy taking what the leadership would consider illegitimate power into their own hands.[3] Table 5 shows that in the years between 1965 and 2002, the proportion of priests believing that premarital sex is always wrong decreased from 80% to 54%. Among the Catholic laity it has decreased from 68% to 16% (NORC General Social Survey, 1972–2000). The conviction that abortion is always wrong has diminished from 91% to 70%. Opposition to birth control as always wrong has fallen from 40% to 27% (from 50% to 12% among the laity). The conviction that masturbation is always wrong has remained

3. A chapter like this one runs the risk of delation to Rome by Catholic reactionaries who believe that he who reports bad news is responsible for it. A Catholic sociologist, they say, should report that people are doing what they should do, not what in fact they are doing—lie, in other words, but only for the good of the Church. I always note in these situations that because I report changes in Catholic moral attitudes does not mean that I approve of them. I do not endorse what happened in the Catholic revolution. But I do believe that it is the duty of a sociologist to protect church leadership from self-deception, that is, from pretending that everything is fine and wonderful when in fact it is not.

Table 5 Priests' Attitudes on Sexual/Gender Issues by Year,
Percentage Who Said It Is Always Wrong

|  | 1965[a] | 1970 | 1993 | 2002 |
|---|---|---|---|---|
| Premarital sex | 80 | 62 | 52 | 54 |
| Abortion |  | 91 | 68 | 70 |
| Birth control | 40 | 29 | 25 | 27 |
| Condoms against AIDS |  |  | 35 | 32 |
| Homosexual sex |  |  | 56 | 50 |
| Artificial insemination |  |  | 47 |  |
| Surrogate mother |  |  | 58 |  |
| Suicide |  |  | 69 | 59 |
| Euthanasia |  |  | 81 |  |
| Pro-choice politicians |  |  | 49 |  |
| Masturbation |  | 29 | 28 | 29 |

*Sources:* Data from NORC study, 1970; Los Angeles Times Poll, 1993; Los Angeles Times Poll, 2002, question 43.
[a] Retrospective question asked in 1970 NORC study.

constant at 29%. However, between 1993 and 2002 opposition to premarital sex, abortion, and birth control have increased by two percentage points because of the influx of a more conservative younger clergy. Opposition by the clergy to homosexual sex has declined to 50%, a few percentage points higher than among the Catholic laity. In 2002 opposition to termination of one's own life declined from 69% to 59%, and in 1993 a little more than half of the priests objected to surrogate motherhood as always wrong and a little less than half thought that artificial insemination was always wrong. Thus at the end of the thirty-eight-year measure, the majority of priests rejected as "always wrong" only abortion and euthanasia, and precisely half thought that homosexual sex is always wrong. (Only 12% of gay priests thought that homosexual sex is always wrong, but only 12% thought it is never wrong as opposed to 2% of the straight priests). Thus, despite the enormous effort brought to bear by church leadership, the Catholic sexual ethic does not enjoy consistent and strong support among most priests. In some matters, however—abortion, birth control, and masturbation—the decline seems to have stopped.

Yet there are signs of recovery of church leaders' authority among those thirty-five and under (5% of the priests) and those between thirty-six and forty-five (17%). The majority in both age groups reject as always wrong both premarital sex and homosexual sex and are in this respect more like the priests over seventy-five than like priests in the middle years of life. The former are a "post-Vatican" generation while the latter are a "pre-Vatican generation" (table 6). However, only approximately two-fifths of these younger cohorts are persuaded that birth control and masturbation are always wrong. Since the birth-control issue has been the touchstone of the restoration of the last three decades, it seems to have failed among the majority of the youngest cohort. Nonetheless, the youngest cohorts are approximately twice as likely as the cohort between fifty-five and sixty-five to think that birth control, masturbation, and premarital sex are always wrong, and more than twice as likely to think that homosexual sex is always wrong. If the generations that come after the youngest cohorts (however small they might be) continue in the same direction, Church leadership will have won at least a partial victory over the Catholic revolution of the late 1960s and early 1970s. Perhaps that victory will spread to the two generations of laity who have grown into adulthood since the rev-

Table 6 Sexual Attitudes by Age, Percentage Who Said It Is Always Wrong

|  | 35 and Under | 36–45 | 46–55 | 56–65 | 66–75 | Over 75 | All |
|---|---|---|---|---|---|---|---|
| Birth control | 39 | 36 | 17 | 16 | 27 | 50 | 28 |
| Masturbation | 44 | 37 | 19 | 16 | 28 | 53 | 28 |
| Premarital sex | 71 | 59 | 46 | 38 | 55 | 73 | 50 |
| Homosexual sex | 72 | 53 | 37 | 19 | 16 | 28 | 50 |

*Source:* Data from Los Angeles Times Poll, 2002, question 43.

olution, though it is unlikely that these younger generations of Catholics, not raised in an era when birth control was deemed by their parents and clergy a serious sin, are now going to accept that it is.

## INTERNAL REFORMS

The key internal reform arguments that have continued through the last several decades are married priests,[4] women priests, and the popular election of bishops (questions 44, 46, and 27 in the *Times* study). About two-thirds of the laity now support these three reforms. In the decade between 1993 and 2002, support among the clergy for married priests increased from 63% to 72%, for the election of bishops from 43% to 46%, and for women priests has remained unchanged at 49%.[5] Forty-two percent would approve even of women bishops and three out of five of women deacons.

Support for ordination of homosexuals stands at 60%. (Homosexual priests are more likely to support all of these changes.) Thus these three reforms continue to enjoy majority support among the laity and substantial support among the clergy, despite the changes that have occurred during the thirty years of restoration. Given the very low

4. The question is usually phrased "ordination of married men," as it is in the studies on which this book is based. Sometimes the wording is "permitting priests to marry." The first wording reflects the practice of Orthodox churches, which ordain married men but do not permit a man to marry after he is ordained. The second wording reflects the Anglican practice of permitting a man to marry (and remarry) both before and after ordination. Most Catholic discussion of the subject assumes the Anglican model.

5. At the time of the 1970 NORC study the majority of priests, still influenced by the hope the Second Vatican Council had created, thought there would be married priests in ten years. Some of those who left to marry said they saw no point in waiting for what would inevitably happen. In 2002 38% thought there would be married priests in the Latin Rite within twenty years. Thirty-five percent thought it would take more than twenty.

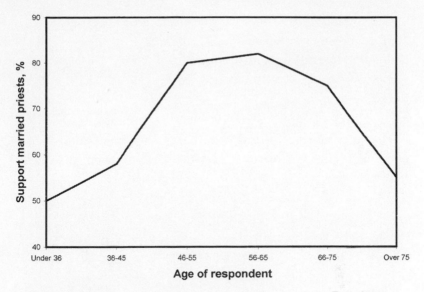

Fig. 3. Support for married priests, by age of respondent. Data from Los Angeles Times Poll, 2002, question 44.

credibility of the clergy and hierarchy at the present time because of the sexual abuse scandal, it does not seem that the laity are likely to change their minds.

However, the striking differences between the younger clergy and the older cohorts persist in this area of reform, too. Figures 3, 4, and 5 illustrate this phenomenon.

Four out of five priests between forty-six and sixty-five support married priests, as do three out of four priests between sixty-six and seventy-five and more than half of those over seventy-five. Even the older men seem to have been won over by the shortage of priests. Nonetheless, only half of the priests thirty-five and under are in favor of married priests, not quite a majority and, as the graph shows, a decline in thirty-five percentage points from the priests in the middle years of life.

Less than 30% of the younger cohort support the ordination of women, accepting the Vatican's decision on this is-

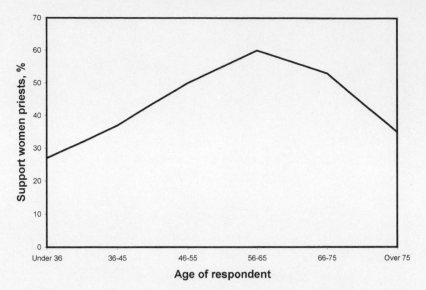

Fig. 4. Support for ordination of women, by age of respondent. Data from Los Angeles Times Poll, 2002, question 46.

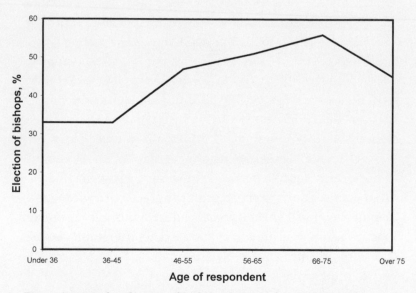

Fig. 5. Support for election of bishops, by age of respondent. Data from Los Angeles Times Poll, 2002, question 27.

sue as definitive, as opposed to more than 60% of those between fifty-six and sixty-five and at least half between forty-six and seventy-five. As in the matter of married priests, the younger cohort are lower in their approval than priests over seventy-five. Finally, only a third of them support election of bishops, as do the majority of priests in the middle years and a near majority of those over seventy-five. Clearly they represent a very different kind of priest, surely more acceptable to the restorationist leadership of the Church, but hardly likely to win friends with their fellow priests or their laity. However, 27% of the priests thirty-five and under would support the ordination of women as bishops.

Who, then, are these young counterrevolutionaries?[6]

In his study of priests ordained five years, Hoge tells us that half believe that the priest is essentially different from the layperson and is a man apart. Thirty-six percent feel that the laity "need to be better educated to respect the authority of the priest's word." They are inclined to be true reactionaries who want to restore, not so much the power that priests had before the Second Vatican Council, but that they had before large numbers of educated Catholic laity emerged after the Second World War. The image that crosses the imagination is the old ethnic monsignors of the Great Depression era.

As I reflect on their responses to Hoge's questions and those of the *Times* surveys, I realize that, in the late 1950s, much of my generation would have agreed with such sentiments. We had the Council ahead of us to jolt us out of our narrowness. These men have come after the Council,

6. I have always tried to resist the propensity to decry the young. One of my seminary mentors, the late Monsignor Ed Roche, warned us of engaging in this scapegoat activity. Once you do that, he asserted, it's a sure sign you're getting old. The data in this essay, however, force me to abandon that policy.

Table 7 Needed Church Reforms by Age, Percentage of Respondents

| | 35 and Under | 36–45 | 46–55 | 56–65 | 66–75 | Over 75 | All |
|---|---|---|---|---|---|---|---|
| None | 17 | 16 | 12 | 7 | 13 | 27 | 14 |
| Liberal | 38 | 37 | 48 | 51 | 45 | 33 | 43 |
| Reactionary | 12 | 11 | 9 | 11 | 12 | 10 | 11 |
| Moderate | 12 | 20 | 17 | 16 | 14 | 8 | 15 |
| Other | 21 | 16 | 14 | 16 | 16 | 21 | 17 |
| Total | 100 | 100 | 100 | 100 | 100 | 100 | 100 |

*Source:* Data from Los Angeles Times Poll, 2002, question 34.

which they did not live through and perhaps do not understand. Older priests complain that younger priests are arrogant, pompous, and rigid, lack theological training, and love to parade in clerical dress. Perhaps these younger men are a result of the successful efforts of the restoration and a new generation of seminary teachers,[7] or perhaps they are a different kind of man than those who used to aspire to the priesthood. Perhaps they are seeking personal security in an old-fashioned clerical caste. Perhaps they are rejecting a world with too much flexibility and not enough certainty. This disconnect may cause an even greater decline of clerical credibility. Their attitudes do make them seem like the kind of priests that church leadership desires today. At a time when it appears that Catholics are drifting away from active religious practice because of the loss of credibility resulting from the sexual abuse scandal, it is difficult to think of this younger generation improving clerical credibility.

The 2002 *Times* study asked an open-ended question about reforms needed in the Church (34). Fourteen percent thought that no reforms were needed at all (table 7).

7. I am told that many come to the seminary with a fully developed rigid theology and hassle instructors who disagree with them and even denounce them to their bishops.

Forty-three percent mentioned reforms that might be characterized as "liberal," continuing the thrust of the Second Vatican Council: concern for the poor, the minorities, empowering the laity, women (1%), celibacy, youth, democracy in the Church, evangelization. Eleven percent listed "reactionary" reforms that included insistence on orthodoxy, elimination of materialism, individualism, abortion, loss of faith, birth control, divorce, the media, anti-Catholicism (the usual jeremiad against the world); 15% "moderate" reforms (such as dealing with the priest shortage and recruiting higher-quality priests); and another 17% a mixture of other reforms. Twenty-nine percent of the younger priests either said there was nothing to reform or endorsed reactionary reforms—which were most often denunciations. Yet 38% of them supported liberal reforms, the smallest in any age category save for those over seventy-five, but still evidence that some of them are indeed influenced by the Council, as are approximately half of those between forty-six and fifty-five. If one lumps the liberal and moderate reforms, approximately two-thirds of priests in the middle years endorse them, as opposed to half of those thirty-five and under. Perhaps emphases on pragmatic reform policies represent the issues on which some of the young may dialogue with their older brothers.

Another open-ended question (28) asked what respondents saw as some of the most serious problems that the Church faced. When the question was worded that way, 22% mentioned some aspect of the sexual abuse problem—credibility, moral problems, quality of clergy, and cover-up. Only 13% of the youngest cohort saw it as a serious problem, as did between a fifth and a fourth of older cohorts. Perhaps members of the youngest cohort do not read the papers or watch TV. Or perhaps they don't take the crisis so seriously because they attribute it all to the media.

Finally for the purpose of this chapter, the respondents were asked to rate the future prospects of the American Church (question 31). Thirty-nine percent describe the prospects as not so good or poor, and 58% urged quick reforms. Those who saw the situation as unpromising were twenty percentage points more likely to think that reforms must be done quickly rather than slowly. The two younger cohorts were the least likely to see urgent reform as important, precisely because they were also the least likely to see prospects as not good or poor. That attitude suggests a group of men who might not have been fully in touch with the situation in 2002.

## SUMMARY

The impetus to reform is still strong in the Catholic Church despite three decades of restoration, at least among those priests who came to maturity during the Second Vatican Council. Priests have not backed off on their attitudes about masturbation, birth control, and premarital sex,[8] and have changed their minds (as have the laity) about homosexual sex and artificial insemination. They also support married priests, the ordination of women (though the Vatican has declared this question "definitively" closed), and the popular election of bishops. The younger cohorts are turning away from these reforms, though the majority of them still believe that birth control and masturbation are not always wrong and advocate the ordination of married men. They are obviously very different from their predecessors and may open up a serious rift in the priesthood in years to come, though it is possible that enough of them may be able to cooperate with their older brothers on prag-

8. I report this fact for the record and reject the interpretation that I approve it.

matic issues. They are, however, very different from the laity, who already do not concede much credibility to the clergy.

Two-fifths of priests think that the condition of the American church is either not too good or poor. This group is much more likely than the optimists to advocate quick reform. The young cohorts are not supportive of quick reform because they are far more optimistic than their older colleagues.

In sum, the conflicts over reform in the Church and the emergence of a largely restorationist younger clergy continue the crisis that began with the convening of the Vatican Council in 1962. It may be that, when the clergy shaped by the Council have all died, the new kind of priest may restore the Church that existed before 1962, the Church structured to resist the French Revolution and the modern world.

By then, it might be a little late.

# 6

## CLERGY, HIERARCHY, AND LAITY

### AN INSTITUTION DEVOID OF TRANSPARENCY?

I f the Church were a business corporation, its priests would be recognized as the lowest level of bureaucrat, men whose job it is to pass management's decisions down to employees and customers. One often hears it said with considerable vigor—by a bishop—that the Church is not a corporation. Perhaps not, yet it often seems that the hierarchy treats priests like low-level employees. Not to be outdone, the clergy often appear to think that the laity are clients for whom one need not have much respect. So, if the Church *were* a business corporation, one might describe it as a dysfunctional firm in which transparency across levels is almost nonexistent, like an airline that is about to go bankrupt.

### POPE AND BISHOPS

Priests appear to rate both the pope and their own bishop favorably on job performance (table 8). However, a little more than half of that approval rating comes from those who say that they "approve somewhat" of the way their bishop handles his duties. Exactly what the word "somewhat" means in that context is difficult to say. It appears to mean that the respondents do not want to say they disapprove of the job performances of their bishop but that they are nonetheless able to contain their enthusiasm. In

Table 8 Attitudes Toward Leaders in 1993 and 2002, Percentage
of Respondents

|  | 1993 | 2002 |
| --- | --- | --- |
| Rate pope favorably | 83 | 88 |
| Rate pope too conservative on moral issues | 41 | 36 |
| Rate bishop favorably | 72 | 79 |
| Rate bishop too conservative on moral issues | 22 | 19 |
| Comfortable in going to bishop or superior with problem | 35 | 36 |

*Source:* Data from Los Angeles Times Poll, 2002, questions 19, 20, and 24–26.

chapter 7 we will see that many priests want to see the bishops who caused the sexual abuse scandal indicted, which demonstrates a lack of confidence in the hierarchy as a whole, if not necessarily in their own bishop.

Moreover, it is difficult to see how those who strongly support the pope and approve his sexual teaching are able nonetheless to disagree with some of the key elements in his sexual teaching. The answer seems to be that they fudge their opposition to, for example, birth control. Those who think that birth control is "never" seriously wrong believe that the pope is too conservative in his sexual teaching. Those who say that birth control is "sometimes" seriously wrong (a hedge of which the pope would surely not approve) are the ones most likely to say that they approve "somewhat" the pope's sexual teaching. By this stratagem they are able to maintain their positive feelings and support for the pope and escape the inconvenience of trying to impose that teaching in the confessional. Since this hedge has been at work now for thirty-five years, it seems unlikely that the strategy will change. Hence the church leadership proclaims a moral regulation at the highest and the intermediate (bishop) levels that the clergy do not try to enforce and that the laity do not obey—with the approval of the lower clergy who have spoken to them for more than three decades about the need and right to follow one's conscience.

Those who approve of their bishop only "somewhat" are also the ones, along with those who don't approve, who are most likely to say that they would not feel free to go to the bishop with a problem. Beneath the support for the leaders, then, is a tendency to fudge and to distrust. The institution is less than transparent. Moreover, it has been that way for at least three decades. Hence the communication system in the Church does not seem to function effectively. How long, one is often asked, can that go on? The answer, based on the long history of the Church, is it could go on for a very long time.

Although we will see later that the ideology of clerical culture strongly endorses mutual support among priests, only a third of priests said (in the 1993 *Times* study) that there was a great deal of support from their fellow priests. Thus many priests are caught in a situation where they are not at ease in confiding to their bishops and experience little support from their fellow priests. Seventeen percent of those who reported loneliness as their most serious problem said they would feel very comfortable speaking with their bishop, as opposed to 37% of those who did not perceive loneliness as a problem.

## PRIESTS AND THE VATICAN

The resistance by priests to demands from the Vatican and from the American hierarchy on sexual issues seems intransigent. Priests have made up their mind about birth control and masturbation, and that would appear to be that, no matter how many solemn pronouncements and instructions come from the Vatican. Such resistance might seem to be almost a principled response (though church leaders would hasten to note that the principles are in error), since only strong convictions would make it possible for priests to systematically ignore authority. One might suspect that among the clergy there is a different theology of human sexuality mixed with a different theory of church authority that underpins their rejection of official church teaching.

At the present there is no possibility of dialogue between the official theory and the de facto theory of priests because church leadership does not engage in dialogues with those who are wrong; indeed, it does not even admit the possibility that those who are wrong might have an inchoate theory that supports their position. Nonetheless, it might be possible with the 1993 data set (when the pertinent questions were all asked) to discover an outline of what seems to be the clerical theory of sex and authority in the Church. Because I attempt to understand the dynamics of clerical resistance to the Vatican's teaching, I reaffirm that it does not follow that as a sociologist I endorse the reasoning—often implicit I suspect—that I am trying to trace. I reject out of hand any charge that I approve (or a charge that I disapprove, for that matter) of this theory. However, I do insist that church leaders would be ill-advised to ignore its prevalence or power.

I speculate that a model composed of four variables might account for much clerical dissent on sexual teaching—support for lay freedom, "liberalism," a positive valuation of sexuality, and a positive valuation of women. The first three variables need little explanation. If priests support lay freedom, such support would certainly include freedom to make their own choices about sexual behavior. Moreover, support for free choice seems to imply a conviction that lay instincts in these matters are to be trusted. In addition, if sexuality is good and not (as St. Augustine thought) just an evil to be tolerated, then priests today would be less likely than their predecessors to condemn all but the most limited forms of sexual pleasure.

The issue of a positive regard for women may be more subtle. Since the time of St. Augustine, a powerful strain of Catholic spirituality has been suspicious of women, because, as Augustine would have it, they destroy the rational self-control of men. In the Middle Ages, friars such as the ineffable John Bromyard warned that women were swamps designed to trap men's souls. They were also compared to tombs filled with corruption and described as allies of the devil. Even in the seminaries of the years immediately before the Second Vatican Council, warnings against the allurements of women were routine before vacations. To a considerable extent, then, the negative Catholic emphasis on sexuality is in fact a negative emphasis on women. Those priests who do not accept such a view of women, I suggest, will be more tolerant of sexual behavior.

There are four items in the 1993 *Times* data that might measure regard for women—support for the ordination of women, support for a condemnation of sexism, support for better ministry to women, and concern for the situation of women religious.[1] Only support for the ordination of women would violate current Vatican teachings. If my speculation is correct, each of these variables should correlate with sexual tolerance. In fact, each of these variables does correlate strongly with tolerance of masturbation, birth control, premarital sex, and homosexuality. The attitudes of priests toward women, then, are crucial to understanding the "theory" that seems to lurk behind their rejection of official teaching. But are these attitudes toward women nothing more than "liberalism"?

I tested my speculations with a five-variable model—

---

1. The first three items were not asked in the 2002 study.

Table 9 Models to Explain Clerical Dissent, Correlations Net
of Impact of All Other Variables

|  | Birth Control | Masturbation |
|---|---|---|
| Age | .06 | .10 |
| "Liberal" | .21 | .21 |
| Would marry | .13 | .12 |
| Regard for women | .18 | .15 |
| Lay freedom | .41 | .36 |
| Variance explained by model | 55% | 49% |

*Source:* Data from Los Angeles Times Poll, 1993.
*Note:* The coefficients are "betas," that is, they show the relationship between a variable and the specific sexual teaching, net of all the other variables in the model put together. Thus respect for lay freedom correlates with attitude on birth control at .41 net of the influence of age, "liberalism," regard for sex, and respect for women.

age, "liberalism" (self-described), support for lay freedom,
positive regard for women (a scale composed of all four
"pro-women" variables), and positive regard for sex (as
measured by the response that the priest would marry if
he were permitted to do so). As table 9 shows, the model is
very powerful in explaining clerical resistance to the official
sexual teaching of the Church—with only age being relatively unimportant. Each of the four other variables is significant and substantial, net of one another. So regard for
women, positive valuation of sex, and respect for lay freedom have an impact of their own above and beyond liberal
ideology. Both the models are substantially more powerful
than one would normally encounter in social research. In
all four variables a positive regard for women continues to
have an important independent effect of its own, no matter
what the moral issue might be. The subtle influence of regard for women cannot therefore be reduced to mere "liberalism."

Nor in 1993 did this regard for women show any sign
of diminishing in the priesthood. More than four out of five
liberal priests under fifty-five are high on the "sensitivity to
women" factor, as are two out of five of the conservatives
in the same age category. The depth and the strength of

clerical resistance to hierarchical teaching cannot be understood without taking the "woman" factor into account.

I trust that it is obvious that I am not suggesting that the indicators of regard for women used in this analysis are the best indicators. They are rather indicators that are available. Nor am I contending that priests have reached satisfactory levels of regard for women. Rather I am saying that younger priests,[2] whether they be "liberals" or "conservatives," have higher regard for women than older priests do and that, however crude the measures available, this regard explains in part why priests resist Vatican orthodoxy on sexual ethics.

## LAITY EVALUATE CLERGY

Before we turn to explicit consideration of what priests think of their laity, it might be appropriate to consider what the laity think of their priests. The first ratings of clerical performance by their laity occurred almost a half century ago in a study by the *Catholic Digest*, which was in fact the first sample survey ever of American religion.[3] At that time 40% of Americans, whether Protestant or Catholic, rated their clergy as excellent in their preaching. Some forty years ago in the NORC parochial school studies, the situation had changed drastically: 40% of Protestants still gave an excellent rating to their clergy, while the Catholic proportion who thought their priests were excellent had fallen to 20%. Subsequent research in the seventies and eighties reported essentially the same finding—though the NORC Young Catholic Adult study reported only a 10% excellent rating among Catholics under thirty.

2. These were the priests thirty-five and under in 1993.
3. The data cards have been missing for years. If anyone has them, please come forward.

Reactions to these findings were underwhelming. Protestants have to be better preachers, it was said, because they don't have the sacraments like we do. Preaching is all the Protestant clergy have to give them, so they better be good at it. We have the Eucharist.

Two studies during the year 2000, however, indicate that Catholics give lower ratings to their clergy across all ministerial activities than do Protestants. The first study was carried out by Knowledge Network (which uses a representative sample of TV sets in the United States), the second was part of NORC's annual General Social Survey (face-to-face interviews of a representative sample). Both samples had approximately 800 respondents. The results of both surveys were similar, increasing confidence in the findings.[4]

Respondents were asked to rate their clergy on a four-point scale (running from "excellent" to "poor") on five (seven in the Knowledge Network study) aspects of clergy performance—preaching, respect for women, sympathetic counseling, working with young people, worship services, and (in the Knowledge Network project) personal warmth and personal joy.

Table 10 shows that Protestants continue to be twice as likely to report that the sermons they hear are excellent. They are also significantly more likely to rate their clergy higher on the other items than are Catholics. Priests do not fare well in evaluations by their laity as compared to Protestant clergy.

Thirty-seven percent of Protestants rate their clergy as excellent in their respect for women, as opposed to 27% of Catholics. The comparison for sympathetic counseling

---

4. I commissioned both of these surveys. In both cases the samples were representative samples of the American population.

Table 10 Rating of Clergy Performance by Religion, Percentage, Who Ranked It Excellent

|  | Protestant | Catholic |
| --- | --- | --- |
| Preaching | 36 | 18 |
| Respect for women | 37 | 27 |
| Sympathetic counseling | 34 | 25 |
| Work with youth | 40 | 28 |
| Worship services | 38 | 28 |
| Personal warmth[a] | 45 | 30 |
| Personal joy[a] | 47 | 31 |

Source: Data from NORC General Social Survey, 2000; Knowledge Network Survey, 2000.
[a] Knowledge Network Survey only.

is 34% versus 25%, for working with young people 40% versus 28%, for worship services 38% versus 28%, for personal warmth 45% versus 30%, and for personal joy 47% versus 31%.

Nor is this evaluation unimportant. Dissatisfaction with your church correlates significantly with low rates of church attendance. When positive attitudes toward the local clergy are taken into account, however, that relationship disappears. It is not the Vatican or the chancery that are important to the laity. It is the performance of the local clergy. To paraphrase Tip O'Neill, all religion is local.

Twenty-seven percent of the Protestants rate their clergy as excellent on at least four items (of the five asked by the General Social Survey) as opposed to 17% of the Catholics. Similarly 24% of the Catholics rate their clergy as fair or poor on at least four items as opposed to 17% of the Protestants. A quarter of the Catholic people think that their priests do a miserable job on almost all of their pastoral activities, and a sixth say that their priests are doing a fine job. Figure 6 shows that only among the oldest laity is approval for priests comparable with Protestant approval for ministers. There is little room for complacency in those findings.

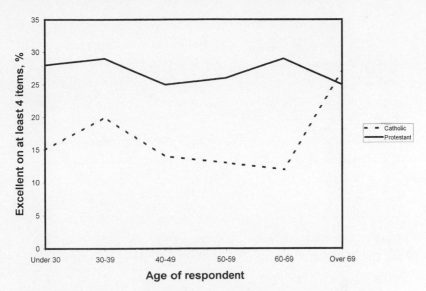

Fig. 6 Rating of clergy as excellent, by age and denomination of respondent. Data from NORC General Social Survey, 2000; Knowledge Network Survey, 2000.

## CLERGY EVALUATE LAITY

The lack of transparency between laity and clergy is illustrated by the fact that in the 2002 study only 19 priests (out of 1,854) responded to the question "What are the greatest problems that the laity you come into contact with face as practicing Catholics?" (38) by saying "bad sermons or liturgy," and only 23 priests pointed at "clericalism." Thirty respondents—in the summer of 2002—mentioned the sexual abuse scandal.

This raises the question of what kind of world priests live in. Anyone who has spent much time in the world of Catholic laity knows that, when the subject of their parish or priests comes up, the conversation turns to the quality of homilies. Only rarely does someone say that they are satisfactory. The laity feel intensely that homilies and liturgy are bad, and the priests don't see preaching as a problem. There is obviously more separating the laity and the clergy than the door to the rectory. Moreover, in the summer of 2002 it seemed impossible not to realize that the sexual abuse scandal was on the minds of almost every Catholic layperson.

How can these things happen? Do priests have extraordinary skills of denial or do they live in a world apart, protected by the vestiges of lay respect that existed a half century ago?

Some priests do stand up for their laity—6% point out that laypeople have been given little power or responsibility in the Church, 2% say that the sexual abuse scandal is a problem for them, another 2% say they have lost confidence in their clergy and bishops, another 1% see bad sermons and liturgy as a problem, and 1% point at "clericalism." Thus some 13% of priests think that the laity might have some legitimate grounds for complaint about clerical ministry. These suggestions are endorsed by 20% of the homosexual priests, by 15% of the priests between forty-five and seventy-five, and by only 7% of those thirty-five and under.

Most priests see the problems of the laity in general descriptive categories that excuse priests from taking any action. Thirteen percent complain that the laity's problems are the result of moral decline (birth control, divorce, abortion, family breakdown, etc.). Ten percent tell us that the laity have lost their faith. Seven percent say that the laity cannot resolve the conflict between their principles and the secular world. Five percent blame apathy, and another 5% blame materialism—those two favorite scapegoats, it would seem, of clerical culture. Four percent report that the laity suffer from the lack of responsibility and personal leadership. Three out of five priests attribute the problems of the laity either to laypeople's own personal failings or to general cultural forces over which the clergy cannot be expected to have any control.

Those Catholic laity who stumble across the previous paragraphs might well find them difficult to believe. Priests really don't have a clue, do they?

Another question (42) produced a similar pattern of responses—"In your opinion, what are the principal reasons laity are leaving the Church these days?"

More than a quarter of priests blame themselves or at least the Church—26% mention such matters as insensitivity, poor leadership, lack of community, something that a priest has done, unfulfilled needs, bad example, intransigence, poor sermons and liturgy, and the sexual abuse scandals. Forty percent of the gay priests mention these clerical faults. Yet priests who work with those who are returning to the Church[5] say that in almost all cases the problem has been something that a priest (or occasionally a nun) has said or done to them in the past, sometimes in the very recent past.

The rest trot out the usual litany of horrors, however: individualism, materialism, secularism, lack of faith, lack of prayer life, lack of commitment, media bias, hedonism, sex, feminism, family breakdown, divorce, lack of education, and apathy. The advantage of this latter group of explanations is that it dispenses priests from any personal responsibility for the departure of Catholics from the Church, and it excuses them from any obligation to respond to the problems. One has the image of the rectory as a fortress island battered by waves of hostile cultural energies against which all it can do is survive.

---

5. Such as Monsignor Tomas O'Cahalaine of the diocese of Tucson, who has formed a program for Alienated Catholics Anonymous in his parish with three six-week sessions every year.

The youngest priests are the least likely to see priests themselves as responsible for the departure of the disaffected laity. Only 16% of them see any priestly responsibility, as do twice as many of those over forty-five.

The picture of priests presented in this analysis is hardly flattering. They seem to have little respect or sympathy for their laity and not much understanding for those who have left the Church. Lay problems are the laity's fault, and lay alienation is their fault, too. At most only a quarter seem sympathetic. How can men, one wonders, who are so happy in their own work have such feelings toward their people? Is it possible that the most serious problem for priests under pressure is not celibacy or homosexuality but the walls of clerical culture, which inure them against the sentiments of their laity, including their feelings about sexual abuse?

One could consider other professions in which the practitioners do not have much respect for their clients yet maintain their standards when dealing with them—medical doctors and police, for example. Patients, we hear, never do what they're told, and the public doesn't obey the police. In practice an individual doctor may still give the patients who take medication irregularly the best possible care, and a cop may be responsible and professional, even with the battered wife who won't bring charges against her abusing husband.

Those who work with people encounter enormous variety in human folly. They need road maps, signposts, simple rough-and-ready explanations that enable them to navigate through the folly of daily life. Shibboleths develop that enable them to sort the crazy Ephraimites, with whom they must cope and perhaps help every day, from the few sensible people that come to their office doors.

"Lack of faith, lack of prayer, lack of responsibility, lack of education, materialism, secularism," etc., etc., are quick and easy answers that the beleaguered cleric tends to give when the random craziness (as it seems to him) of his daily work seems to close in on him. The angry and crazy laity who assail him can be branded with one or the other of these labels, as can those surly and nasty folks who have walked out on him and the Church.

Yet these clichés of clerical culture won't do. They suggest that many, many priests have no idea of the spiritual needs and the spiritual problems of the laity and are all too ready to push them into simple categories that ease priests' workload and, worse, deaden their ability to be sympathetic. Priests are not the only ones who use stereotypes to organize the world. Given who and what they are or are supposed to be, however, one might hope that they would display more sensitivity in their rough-and-ready descriptions of their own people.

I confess I don't understand fully the intricate tangle of shibboleths, denials, and avoidance that produces the evaluations of the laity reported in this and previous chapters, a tangle that is supported by most priests. Perhaps, deep down, many clerics are aware of the glaze of boredom that slips over the faces of the congregation when priests mount the pulpit and would rather not admit how bad they are at what is their most important work of the week.

# 7

## PRIESTS UNDER PRESSURE

The spring and summer of 2002 was a difficult time for priests, or should have been difficult. They were under constant assault from the media because of what often seemed to be a contagion of child abuse (though most of the reports were of events that happened long ago). Inside the Church the "liberals" were blaming sexual abuse on celibacy, and the conservatives were blaming it on homosexuality, neither with much more in the way of evidence than strong personal opinions. From being one of the most respected of professions, the priesthood became a subject for Jay Leno jokes and *New Yorker* cartoons. The bishops met in Dallas and, frightened by the anger of the laity and the threat of huge suits, adopted a reform program that seemed draconian. "Victims"—self-anointed leaders of victim groups—denounced the reform program as inadequate. Some priest leaders argued that the bishops had sold them out and deprived them of their rights. Then the Vatican reviewed the Dallas proposals with a demand for modifications (which in fact were minor), and the battle began all over again. Many priests, if one were to believe the stories, were reluctant to appear in public in their Roman collars—so dearly loved by the restorationists in the younger clergy (who apparently have never seen any pictures of nineteenth-century bishops and priests in Ireland and the United States).

In 1993 46% of priests thought that sexual abuse was a

serious problem, 60% thought that the Church had been too lenient in the past, and 93% thought that the present procedures for dealing with the problem were sufficient.[1] In a certain sense they were right. After Cardinal Joseph Bernardin introduced his reforms in Chicago[2] many other dioceses introduced similar reforms. It appeared that the sexual abuse problem had been solved. Unfortunately some dioceses, especially around Boston and New York, rejected the Bernardin plan (which had been sent to every bishop in the United States), and the explosions in New England brought the issue back into the national agenda. Cardinal Law, who apparently campaigned actively against the Bernardin reforms as "anti-clerical," and his cronies did an excellent job of causing trouble for the whole American church, including those dioceses that had instituted a plan to cope with the problem. The optimism in the 1993 study might have seemed justified; however, priests had changed their mind by 2002: 65% at that time disapproved of the way the bishops had handled the problems (question 59 of the *Times* study). However, only 19% believe that most charges are true, and some 42% more think that many of them are true (question 60). Thirty-eight percent think that only some or none are true. It would appear that most priests even in the summer and autumn of 2002 were still in a state of denial and do not understand the horror of the abuse of the victim and the victim's family. In 1970 and 1993 priests tended to reject all serious charges against a person they knew. The recent crisis has not forced them to give up their denial. The National Federation of Priests' Councils still laments the suffering of accused priests.

1. Including 95% in Boston.
2. In which twenty-three priests were removed from office and a lay-dominated fitness review board was established.

Repeating the question (61) of 1993, 53% thought in 2002 that the Church had been too lenient in the past, and 39% reported that they were either mostly or somewhat satisfied with the Dallas reforms (62). Fifty-five percent thought that the bishops had done a good job in Dallas in restoring public confidence, and 72% thought they had done a good job in protecting minors from abuse (question 63). Only 33% thought the bishops had been fair to accused priests, and only a third agreed strongly that the sexual abuse scandal was the most serious crisis in the history of the American church (65; one wonders what was more serious).

When asked what troubled them most about the allegations of abuse (66), only 5% said that it was the suffering of the victims. Seventeen percent were troubled by the responsibility of the bishops and 10% by the quality of media coverage. Six percent were dismayed by the cover-up by bishops and another 6% by the Church's responsibility. Eleven percent were upset by the fact that the charges were unsubstantiated and 6% by the loss of the credibility of the Church. Three percent were troubled by the sins of priests. Only five respondents saw any trace of personal responsibility of priests revealed at Dallas.

It would appear that the respondents in the 2002 study tend to wash their hands of personal responsibility. You blame bishops and the whole Church and the media and the cover-up and the reassignment, and you worry about false charges and the greed of lawyers, and you regret the loss of credibility, but not many of you feel any personal responsibility and only 5% of you worry about the suffering of the victims.

You don't ask yourself how many times you knew or suspected that something bad was going on in a rectory or how often you demonized a victim and his family or blamed lawyers for causing the problem or how often you insisted that in a given case the priest was innocent. Had he not denied the charges? Had not the doctors and the police cleared him? How often did you admit even to yourself that maybe you were kidding yourself because of loyalty to the priesthood? So, of the various characters involved in the tragedy, the bishops and the media and the victims and the lawyers did bad things. But not priests. Forty-one percent want the responsible bishops to resign, and 11% want them to be indicted and sent to jail (question 67).[3] But not the priests who might have cooperated in the cover-ups and certainly not those who knew deep down inside that something was wrong and did not speak up.

We have been innocent all along and so, priests will still tell you, are a lot of the accused priests.

One wonders about the psychology behind such denials. Do the police who lie to protect the others in the "thin blue line" really believe their denials? Does what begins as a lie become transformed to the truth? Or does the conviction that they must defend one of their own preclude them from accepting the possibility that their colleague might be responsible for criminal misbehavior?

I don't know the answer to that question. Nor do I know how much dishonesty and how much denial exists in the defense by priests of sexual abusers. Are the rules of clerical culture so strong that priests are really blind to the possibility of abuse, that they can't see it when it's there?

Thus, if priests are under pressure, they don't seem to notice it and they certainly are not about to assume personal responsibility for the pressure or for turning down the heat. I know of no priest association in the country that has created an ethical practices committee to engage in self-policing and the enforcement of professional practices. It

3. Not bad ideas.

is not our job, they say, it's up to the police and the bishops and the lay review boards to do something about the sexual abuse problem, if indeed there is a problem.

They really don't get it, not even now. Sermons and liturgy are not serious problems, nor are priests in even a remote way responsible for the sexual abuse crisis. Their hands are clean. They just want to make sure that their own rights are defended if they are unjustly accused.

I suspect that many priests had to know what was happening but couldn't admit it to themselves for years, even decades, because of the norms of clerical culture. Nor can they admit the problem of poor homilies and liturgy because that would betray their fellow priests who do not preach well. The oft-heard explanation, "Well, he can't preach very well, but the people admire his holiness and his care for the sick," is dishonest because it ignores the basic Christian insight that the laity have the right to hear the Gospel preached to them, a right that seems to apply only to the Protestant laity. Blaming the media and blaming lay apathy are a denial of the fundamental problem of priestly ministry: many priests are not very good at what they're supposed to be doing.

The problems in the priesthood come from neither celibacy nor homosexuality. The problems come rather from the iron law of denial and silence that clerical culture imposes on priests.[4] Like many other small groups doing difficult work under trying circumstances, and fearing enemies beyond the boundaries of the group, priests have created an amalgam of norms, beliefs, and practices to protect themselves (and the Church, as they would see it) from their enemies. Protestants, "non-Catholics," and the laity

4. The following paragraphs are a phenomenological description of clerical culture by one who likes priests but can't stand clergy.

must not know about our drunks, our borderline personalities, our loafers, our slugs, our eccentrics, our womanizers, our strange ones that dote on little boys or little girls, and all the other men who somehow managed to make it to ordination.[5] To keep this systematic denial effective, we sometimes have to blind ourselves to the obvious.

We have gone through seminaries at the same time (and often the same seminaries). We have been together for years. We have fought the good fight. We were together on St. Crispin's Day. We are a band of brothers, the happy few. We spend our vacations together. We take days off together. We eat dinners together. We speak the same kind of clergy lingo. We know the same jokes. We share the same gossip.

Our closest friends are priests, as are our most intimate confidants. We take care of one another when we're sick. We give each other loans when we need it. We listen to one another's problems and complaints. We reassure one another. We grieve with one another. We stand at one another's death bed. We priests stick together, even when some of us are no longer active in the ministry. We celebrate our anniversaries together, often these days with our married classmates and their spouses.

I condemn none of these customs nor the intense loyalty that supports them. Nonetheless, when other priests are our only friends, when networks of priests are the primary source of close relationships, when the values of our fellow clergy create our only perspectives on the world, when gos-

5. When I began to write about the sexual abuse problem in 1985, a priest stopped by to argue that I should stop it. "Aren't you just providing ammunition for the Protestants who have been saying these things about us for years?" The issue was not whether I was writing the truth. He knew as well as I did that it was true. Another priest phoned me, a man with simple but sincere pieties (and an Irish brogue). "Father, even if the things you say are true, have you forgotten that those men are *PRIESTS?*"

sip about other priests is our principal subject for small talk, we are isolating ourselves—and dangerously so—from the rest of humankind.

Eugene Cullen Kennedy sees this band-of-brothers interpersonal network as an unhealthy result of celibacy and the patriarchal structure of the church, precisely, it would seem, because it is celibate. Undoubtedly the fact that priests do not have wives or children of their own does mean that they invest more of their emotions in friendships, especially with men who share the same work and the same ideals. Yet male bonding is not considered unhealthy in itself. One can only make the case that these relationships are unhealthy when they cut priests off from most other relationships and limit their perspectives to those of the clerical caste—which means their opinions are often expressed in similar clichés (like "apathy," "materialism," "secularism"). Other ministerial groups and law-enforcement groups have similar networks, mitigated somewhat by the fact that the men are usually married.[6] Alas, the propensity to make too much of this good of friendship among priests can easily seal men up in a hermetic world from which they rarely escape and whose walls, however invisible, are a dense barrier to sensitivity toward other worlds. Hence many priests are not really

---

6. A tragic story about priests standing by other priests: In the early 1980s the *Chicago Sun Times* began a series of articles about the finances of Cardinal Cody. Most priests in Chicago knew enough about the cardinal's wheelings and dealings to suspect that the articles were probably true (which they were). Nonetheless, they condemned the series and attacked the paper and the reporters. One reporter, a devout Catholic, went into his parish church on Sunday and heard himself condemned from the altar by his pastor. The priest, who was one of the admired giants of the archdiocese, surely knew better. Yet he had to defend his archbishop, with the theme that the "cardinal had done so much for the poor." The reporter died the following year at the age of fifty. His family has always believed that the Cody stories and the denunciation by his pastor had cut short his life. When a cardinal is attacked by the media, he becomes "one of the guys."

concerned about the victims of sexual abuse, because they lack empathy for such suffering, as well as because they resent the charges the victim has brought against one of the band of brothers.

In the years when my generation was in the seminary, we were urged to associate on vacation only with other seminarians and after ordination only with other priests. It was only when I went to graduate school six years after ordination that I began to realize that there were other people with whom I had more in common than I did with my seminary classmates—though the latter will always be special people for me.

The seminary ideology said that the priesthood was the great fraternity of men who always stood by one another in time of trouble. That assertion I think is generally true except in one circumstance. If a priest is successful beyond certain very narrow limits or is seen as successful, then he is in real trouble. The clerical culture imposes stern limits on how different one should be from other priests. If you are really loyal to your brothers, you do not embarrass them by proving that you can do something they can't do. If a priest gets a reputation for being a good preacher, for example, it is likely to be held against him by some of his colleagues.[7] Clerical culture has a paradigm for responding to that problem. When a layman mentions to a priest that Father X is a good preacher, the response is likely to be, "Yes, he preaches very well, but he doesn't get along with kids." Or "He's really good, but all he does during the week is prepare his sermon." Or "Everyone says that and it's probably true, but he's not an easy man to live with."

The format of praise mixed with a knife in the back is

7. Nothing worse can happen to a priest, especially a younger priest, than to have parishioners call to ask what time he is saying Mass.

assumed to be effective and it often is. Some laity see through it, however.

Thus to be a member of clerical culture in good standing, a priest must try not to be too good at anything or to express unusual views or to criticize accepted practices or even to read too much. Some ideas are all right, but too many ideas are dangerous.

## BISHOPS ARE PRIESTS TOO

Bishops are priests too and part of clerical culture, though they are the power centers within it. Thus a bishop can reprimand a priest by saying, "Do you know what your fellow priests are saying about you?" Or "Why are you embarrassing other priests by writing what you write?" I'm told that line still works.

Because they are priests, however, bishops are also committed to the norm that, although you may knock down a priest who seems to be too successful, you take care of priests when they are in trouble. Generally bishops are gracious and generous to men who are leaving the priesthood, to drunks, to the emotionally troubled, to the confused, to the unhappy, and to those whom they think might have been falsely accused.

It was precisely this conviction, that one must be gracious to priests, that led Cardinal Law to oppose Cardinal Bernardin's reforms as "anti-clerical." Clearly Cardinal Law was trapped in clerical culture.

No one can rightly criticize episcopal kindness. However, many bishops have extended their generosity to accused abusers. Thus, when one reads transcripts of the memos or the testimony of Cardinal Law or Cardinal Egan, one must understand that both men are priests honoring the code of loyalty to members of their brotherhood. This is not an excuse for their behavior, but merely an attempt to put it in the context of the ideology of clerical culture. Cardinal Egan wrote sympathetically that a Bridgeport priest whom he reassigned was "graceful." No one had told him that most abusers are charming men and graceful liars. Abusers often seem to their friends to be "one of the guys." You stand by one of the guys even if you are a bishop.[8]

Hilaire Belloc, an English Catholic writer from the first half of the last century, once remarked apropos of Catholic leadership that any organization whose leadership was guilty of such knavish imbecility must have the special protection of God. Yet one must wonder why. Why did some church leaders fall victim to the current wave of knavish imbecility? How could they possibly believe, a lawyer asked me, that in the age of the copier and an aggressively inquisitive media anything could be kept secret?

Some "experts" appeal to celibate clerical culture as an explanation, with no evidence to support such an argument and no explanation of why police, physicians, and sometimes academics similarly protect their own. So do many church leaders of other denominations, though not with so much dedicated imbecility.

A bishop is under pressure to exercise paternal care of the priest in trouble. The bishop finds himself inclined to the same denials and demonization as other priests: maybe the charges are not true, maybe the so-called victims brought it on themselves, maybe they're just interested in money, maybe the priest deserves another chance. The police have not brought charges; the doctors offer ambiguous advice; the lawyers think they can fend off a suit. The media thus far have left these events alone. The priest vigorously denies that he ever touched the alleged victim. Just one more chance. Many bishops, perhaps most bishops,

8. Cardinal Egan is far too refined to use the word "guy."

even the most churlish, feel a compulsion to be kind to the priest in trouble. (There but for the grace of God.) So they beat up on the victims and their families and send the man off to an institution and then, hoping he's cured, send him back to a parish. We have covered up before and got away with it, have we not? What reason is there to think that we can't continue to do so? Perhaps there have been some lies, but only for the good of the Church.

Should a trial materialize, the bishops, trapped between adversarial lawyers ("the victims and their families are the enemy") and their own doubts about the guilt of the priest ("he still denies it"), are willing (as was Bishop Edward Egan in Bridgeport) to argue through lawyers that priests do not work for the church but are independent contractors. Or they argue, as Cardinal Anthony Bevilacqua did through his lawyers in Philadelphia, that the victims' parents are legally responsible for not warning their child of the dangers.

This is the slippery slope that begins with loyalty to a fellow priest, doubt about guilt, and paternalist duty to be kind and ends either with reassignment or hardball litigation. At every step of the way, the bishop's advisers encourage him to give the priest another chance or to fight back.[9] The kind of men who are made bishops today find it difficult simply to dump a fellow priest, and, similarly, their advisers find it difficult to suggest doing so (though in Boston, Bishop John Michael D'Arcy did indeed give such advice).

This narrative might suggest some sympathy for the decisions many bishops made. But I am attempting to under-

9. Some lawyers have advised bishops that their personal records are in fact owned by the Vatican and hence protected by diplomatic immunity. Those whom the gods would destroy they first make mad.

stand and explain, not to defend. The decisions made across the country are manifestations of knavish imbecility. Yet I can understand how men could have made them.

Mistakes were perhaps understandable before 1985, when at their meeting at St. John's Abbey the bishops heard for the first time a systematic presentation about child abuse that told them that it is not a spiritual problem that can be cured by prayer and willpower, but an emotional illness for which the recidivism rate is almost 100%. They became less understandable after 1993, when the hierarchy put together a perfectly reasonable set of guidelines (which were systematically ignored) and when Cardinal Joseph Bernardin distributed copies of his policies in Chicago to every bishop in the country.

It must have been very hard for Joseph Bernardin, the kindest and gentlest of men, to remove more than twenty priests from active ministry. The Chicago system does not work perfectly; no system could. But it works better than anything that seems to have functioned for the last ten years in the Northeast. As far as I am concerned, the statute of limitations on knavish imbecility ended in 1992. Bishops who reassigned abusive priests after the early nineties were, according to the traditional norms of Catholic morality, guilty of grave sin.

There were three sins. First, they besmirched the office of bishop and seriously weakened its credibility. Second, they scandalized the Catholic laity, perhaps the worst scandal in the history of our republic. But their gravest sin was not to consider the victims, not even to talk to the victims and their families, to blind themselves to the terrible wreckage that sexual abuse causes for human lives. Bishops worried about their priests; they did not worry about the victims. They did not seem to understand that, as the laity would later see it, at the same time they were trying to inhibit sexual satisfaction in the marital bed, they were facilitating sexual satisfaction for abusive priests.

When I argue that many Catholic leaders have sinned, I am not judging the state of their conscience. I do not have the gift of reading of hearts (*scrutatio cordilim*). I will leave it to God to judge their moral responsibility. I am merely saying that, by cooperating with the sexual abuse of children and young boys, they were objectively sinning—and it is hard to see how they can claim invincible ignorance. They were, in fact, according to the strict canons of the old moral theology, necessary cooperators in evil and objectively as responsible for the evil as those who actually did it.

When I began to play my quixotic game on child abuse, I was astonished to discover how powerful were the denial mechanisms. The evidence against some of the men was overwhelming. Moreover, other priests knew vaguely what was happening. Yet they vigorously and angrily denied the charges. "The doctors and the cops have cleared him." They hadn't really. Note that it was virtually the same sentence that Cardinal Law would use about a priest he had reassigned. They hadn't really in that man's case either. But presumably Cardinal Law wanted to believe, just as Chicago priests wanted to believe, in the innocence of their accused brother.

## DENIAL AMONG PRIESTS

Walls of denial that thick can easily account for how clueless priests are about the lay evaluation of their professional behavior. They tune out lay dissatisfaction easily because of the remnants of the old respect for the clergy.[10] No one

10. "Poor Father was sick again this morning" was once a useful phrase for daily Mass goers, who meant, "He's hungover again!"

dares walk up to a parish priest after Mass and say something like, "That may have been the worst homily you have ever delivered, and you've delivered a lot of bad homilies." Or "I've been to dull and lifeless baptisms before, but this one hits a new low."

The laity therefore cooperate in the poor service of the clergy. Even if they write a letter of complaint to the bishop, they must not forget that the bishop is a priest too and is likely to stand by one of the guys.

It is important that priests join forces with one another and with the hierarchy and the laity in eliminating child abuse. It is also important that they join forces to break through the thick veils of clerical culture and improve their ministerial skills, perhaps by listening to the laity, even seeking their help.

# 8

## CONCLUSIONS

1. A. W. Richard Sipe's contention that the sexual revolution outdates the 1970 NORC study is not supported by the evidence. That study may still be used to make population estimates about priests. While it would be useful to replicate that study and combine it with data about the parishes in which the priest respondents work, it is unlikely that anyone would be willing to pay for such a project.

2. Nor is there any support in the data for the arguments of Sipe and Eugene Cullen Kennedy that priests are emotionally immature. Quite the contrary: the continuity between the Personality Orientation Inventory data from 1970 and the Thomas Nestor data from 1993 indicates that priests on the average continue to be as mature and as capable of intimacy as married laymen. Celibates, contrary to the media's conventional wisdom, are not on the average incomplete and inadequate human beings, or at least no more so than other men. Indeed, they are more likely to be satisfied with their work and their lives than are married Protestant clergy.

3. Most priests are celibate heterosexuals. Approximately one out of six priests is homosexual, and most homosexual priests are celibate. There is no support in the data for plans to exclude homosexuals from the seminary or to bar them from the priesthood. Only one out of ten of them believes that homosexual sex is never wrong. They appear to be more sensitive to the needs and feelings of the

laity and more open to reforms like the popular election of bishops. Homosexual subcultures seem to be prevalent in both seminaries and dioceses. Because some few abusing priests are celibates, it does not follow that all celibates are abusers. Because some few abusers are homosexual, it does not follow that all homosexuals are abusers. Attempts to blame abuse on either celibacy or homosexuality are defamatory. The logic of such accusations is to be found not in rationality but in angry ideology and anti-Catholic bigotry.

4. There is no evidence in the data to support the argument of writers like Kennedy and Sipe that priests on the average are unhappy misfits. Quite the contrary: despite their celibate state, they are among the happiest men in the world. They say that they would become priests again, that they are satisfied in the priesthood, that the priesthood is better than they expected, and that they are not thinking of leaving the active ministry. On such measures their average scores are higher than those of the married Protestant clergy.

5. The desire to marry by itself accounts for about one out of six defections from the active ministry. In the absence of dissatisfaction with the priesthood (a respondent would not choose to be a priest if he had it to do over again), only a few men would leave the active ministry. While a case can be made for the abolition of celibacy because of low recruiting rates into the priesthood, the data do not support the claim that celibacy is driving most of those who leave out of the priesthood.

6. Priests stay in the priesthood and are happy in the ministry because they like being priests. They like being priests because they like the things priests do. They are on average religious altruists, however, not just social workers or social justice activists. It is hard for many, both inside the Church and outside, to comprehend that a man can be

a happy, fulfilled, and mature human being without a woman of his own. However, celibate priests prove that this is possible and rewarding.

7. The younger generation of priests (under forty-five) are on average very different from their predecessors. Some of them may be seeking the security that comes from a position of status and power and appear to be narrow and inflexible. Half of them, in Dean Hoge's work, believe that priests are essentially different from the laity, and more than a third insist that the laity must be educated to recognize the authority of a priest's word. There is no reason to think that they will not encounter conflict with older clergy and the laity.

8. Most priests do not accept the Church's sexual teaching. On the crucial issues of birth control and masturbation even the youngest cohorts do not accept the teaching that these behaviors are always wrong. This dissent, persistent now for over thirty years, can be traced to an ideology based on respect for women and respect for the freedom of the laity.

9. Most priests support the ordination of married men and the election of bishops. About half also support the ordination of women. Even the youngest cohorts approved the ordination of married men. Almost two out of five expect a change within the next twenty years. Two-fifths approve the election of women bishops.

10. Priests are surprisingly insensitive to their laity. Most priests dismiss them as lacking in faith, spirituality, and prayer life as well as being victims of apathy, materialism, secularism, and individualism. Very few priests seem to sense that the laity are massively dissatisfied with the quality of priestly ministry (which indeed they are). The walls that clerical culture establishes between the laity and the clergy appear to impede communication between the

two groups. This clerical culture is less a negative effect of celibacy (as Kennedy insists) than a male-bonding, band-of-brothers phenomenon that has gone too far. It might be a path-determined relic of the past[1] that impedes the effectiveness of ministry, perhaps in part from penal times in Ireland.

11. While priests may be under pressure because of the sexual abuse crisis, they did not seem in the summer and autumn of 2002 to think that it was all that serious. Neither did they seem to realize that it is a monumental problem for their laity. If it is a problem at all, it was not *their* problem. The bishops and the media are responsible for the crisis, and the bishops must do something about it. Indeed the majority of priests (like the laity) want the bishops who caused the problem to resign. Some even want them to be indicted and sent to jail. They are persuaded, however, that the new reform plans will probably work—just as they were in 1993.

12. Clerical culture also may explain how so many bishops could have had blinders on about the abuse problem even in the middle and late 1990s. Like all priests, bishops feel strong bonds of loyalty to priests. This loyalty causes them to deny what seems obviously true to others.

1. The inertial result of structures established long ago and reinforced repeatedly ever since.

# 9

## POLICY IMPLICATIONS

I t is expected of someone who writes about a social problem that he make policy recommendations for dealing
with the problem. I will respond to this expectation, so long
as it is understood that my recommendations are my own
reflections on the data and do not flow logically from the data.
Also, I want it understood that I do not deceive myself that
anyone—priest, bishop, curialist—will take them seriously.

### HOMOSEXUAL PRIESTS

There is nothing in this book that justifies the hysteria
among some Catholics on the subject of homosexual
priests. Nor is there anything that will persuade the Vatican
that homosexuals should not be banned from seminaries
and the priesthood. The fury of the homophobia in the
Church will not yield to data. It would be a wise policy for
church leaders to tone down the hysteria and leave homosexual priests alone, so long as they avoid the gay "scene"
and the gay "lifestyle." Yet perhaps priests who are homosexual should avoid blatant manifestations of homosexual
friendship groups, which create the impression of homosexual subcultures. On the other hand, they are entitled to
have friends who share similar problems.

### CELIBACY

Patently, most men who leave the priesthood do not leave
because of celibacy. They must also dislike the work of the

priest to the extent that they say they would not choose again to be a priest. Despite the happiness and maturity of most celibate priests, few of them are willing to speak out in its defense. Hence there is little resistance to the constant propaganda that celibates are inadequate human beings and that celibacy causes child abuse. The proper response to these attacks would have to come from priests themselves and especially from the organized priest groups such as the National Federation of Priests' Councils. Yet these groups are committed to the abolition of the celibacy rule and apparently think that to defend celibacy would be to insult those who have left the active ministry. If priests are unwilling to defend their collective reputation, then there is no reason to think that anyone else will.

## VOCATIONS TO THE PRIESTHOOD

There seems to be broad agreement among priests that the ordination of married men is the only solution for the shortage of priests. There is no evidence to support this confidence, nothing to prove that there are thousands of married men who would be qualified to be priests if only they could bring their wives along. Indeed, one must wonder about the man who is ready to bring his wife and children into such a dysfunctional institution as the Catholic Church in the United States is today. Moreover, is it really true that celibacy is what is keeping young men away from seminaries? Everyone seems to believe that this is true, so there is no ground for seeking proof. Yet, in principle, another explanation might be possible. Perhaps young men are not seeking out the priesthood because no one is trying to recruit them.

In the Knights of Columbus study of Catholic young people made in the late 1970s, my colleagues and I discovered that nine out of ten of our male respondents who expressed some interest in the priesthood had never been approached by any priest on the subject. If only a small proportion of those young men had become priests, there would be no priest shortage today. But why, if priests are so happy and so satisfied in the priesthood, if celibacy is not a serious problem for most of them, and if even those who would like to marry remain in the priesthood because they like it even more than they think they would like marriage, are priests so reluctant to engage in vocational recruiting?

The answer to that question, it appears to me, is to be found in a problem that social scientists call pluralistic ignorance. Most priests as individuals are happy as priests, but they do not think others are happy. As individuals they do not find celibacy a serious personal problem. But most priests (it would appear) believe that the majority of their fellow priests are unhappy because for them celibacy is a serious personal problem. The reason is that at most gatherings of priests the lowest common denominator of envy, misery, and mediocrity tends to dominate the conversation. Hence the astonishment among many priests at the findings I reported from the first *Los Angeles Times* study. Astonishment and blunt denial.

Priests tell me that they simply will not try to recruit young men into a group where morale is so low and where there is so much dissatisfaction unless and until the Church changes the celibacy rule. In effect they are engaging in a game of chicken with the Vatican, defying the Holy See to change the celibacy rule or run out of priests—behavior that, for whatever my opinion might be worth, is immature and self-defeating. As we say in Chicago, go fight city hall!

The vocation crisis may be a matter of smoke and mirrors. But the smoke and mirrors have a very real consequence—an ever-increasing shortage of priests. Whence the destructive smoke and mirrors? I suggest that they come from the loud attacks on the current condition of the priesthood by a small minority of former priests, by the tiny minority of active priests who are unhappy, and by the anger of some members of the lay elite. Those who are happy in the priesthood and those who understand and apparently embrace celibacy have been intimidated into silence by the anticelibacy crusade. They are afraid to say publicly that they find the priesthood better than they expected because they might hurt the feelings of their former colleagues and have their masculinity or humanity questioned by an articulate minority of resigned priests and by lay elite who perceive celibacy as an attack on the equal virtue of married sexuality.

On this subject, doubtless some religion teachers, vocation directors, and retreat masters preached not so long ago that abstinence is something intrinsically superior to sexual experience. But I doubt that most priests believe that. Even in the reactionary seminary I attended (twenty-five years ahead of its time, it was said, because it responded to the problems of 1850 with the answers of 1875), this notion was not part of the ethos. Perhaps the vehemence of the anticelibacy among some laypeople is a result of their anger at the way the Church has meddled in their sexual lives, a valid anger no doubt, but aimed at the wrong target, because since 1965 the celibate parish clergy has been on their side.

However, I do not blame the vocation shortage on the anticelibacy ideology and its assault on those who remain in the priesthood and who dare to defend celibacy. Laypeople have reason to be angry even if they choose the wrong target. Former priests who have suffered have the right to speak out about their sufferings and attack what they think was the cause of their suffering.

The real cause of the vocation shortage is the reticence of those who are happy in the priesthood and not excessively burdened by celibacy. They may complain about the shortage of priests, but they are not ready yet to do battle with the anticelibacy ideologues, to recruit young men to what is a happy and satisfying life. Nor are they ready to speak, individually or collectively, about the joys of being a priest, joys about which there can be no doubt after studying the results of the two *Times* studies.

If the celibacy rule is abolished, fine. But let it be abolished for good reasons—that it is right and proper and good for married men to be in the priesthood, not because celibacy has driven out of the priesthood most of those who have left and not because celibacy as such is the cause of the vocation crisis. These two reasons are nothing more than smoke and mirrors. Moreover, they are false prophecies and those who proclaim them false prophets.

I have advocated for three decades the establishment of a Priest Corps, something like the Peace Corps—a group of young men who are willing to commit themselves to a limited term of service to the Church in the priesthood, say five or ten years, renewable. If they like being priests—and the evidence in these studies suggests that they would—then they may want to stay. If not, then they are free to go, with gratitude and respect. The merit of this modest proposal is that it makes a virtue out of present necessity. Men now do feel free to leave the priesthood if they are not happy in it. Unfortunately their treatment by the Church is disgraceful. My Priest Corps scheme would merely require that the Church treat them honorably and that there would be periodic moments when they could review and renew their commitment. Theologically, they might still be priests and even be called on occasionally to exercise ministry. In practice they would be men who serve generously for a time and go on to other careers.

The ideologues on both sides of the celibacy debate dismiss this proposal as a "compromise." The Church must either defend celibacy in "this time of testing" or abolish it entirely. We must not tolerate experiments with some kind of "middle way."

In the first hundred years of the priesthood in Chicago, the average age of a priest at the time of his death was thirty-six. For most of human history most men (priests or not) were dead by the time they were forty. Now the majority of priests live to their golden jubilee. This demographic revolution transforms completely the ambience of priestly commitment. If a man approaching the age of forty cannot stand teenagers, grows weary of the bedlam of the rectory office, finds most other priests insufferable, and would like to take unto his bed a wife and to begin a family of his own, what useful purpose for the man or for the priesthood or for the Church is served by trying to prevent his departure? What good does it do to force a deeply unhappy man to stay in the priesthood?

As for the young man who might like to be a priest but finds celibacy a daunting prospect and has heard all the anticelibacy diatribes, could one not say to him, "Give it a try till you're thirty-five or forty, and if you want to reconsider then, it would be fine with us."

Would it not be better to experiment with such a program before attempting to reverse a thousand years or so of history?

## RECENTLY ORDAINED PRIESTS

There can be no objection to a newer cohort of priests that does not accept the conventional wisdom of its predecessors. However, one can and should object to those in the newer cohort who are inflexibly resistant to the acquisition of any new knowledge and who have made up their mind what kind of priest they're going to be even before they arrive at the seminary. Not all of the younger priests are of that sort, but some apparently are. Seminary authorities should hesitate before recommending the ordination of such a man, as hesitant as they would be about the ordination of someone who frequents gay bars or who shows sign of being a child abuser. The Church always needs new men with vigor and zeal and new ideas. But the Church no more needs a subculture that demands lay submissiveness and seeks comfort and security from clerical status than it needs a subculture that is openly and flagrantly gay.

## PRIESTLY SERVICE
## AND CLERICAL CULTURE

The findings reported in this study about the inadequacies of priestly service and negativity of clergy reaction to their laity are arguably the most serious problems that the priesthood faces. How can mature men, happy in their priestly commitment and determined to remain in the priesthood, be sloppy in their professional activities and dismissively contemptuous of their laity? The protective structures of the clerical caste must be broken open, and authentic and honest communication between the laity and their clergy must begin. It is intolerably tragic that a cultural system should block the effective ministry of men who have given up much to be priests.

What is to be done?

The seminaries must face the fact that they are not turning out well-trained professional clergy. They must realize that preaching is creative work and that some element of creativity should be required as a condition for ordination.

No one should be ordained who has not done some kind of creative exercise—a short story, a cycle of poems, an art or photo exhibit.[1]

Bishops must realize that it is idle to babble about evangelization when those in the neighborhoods who are supposed to evangelize do not, on the average and with some happy exceptions, do a very good job at it.

The priest organizations around the country, both local and national, should realize that their membership has a serious image problem and undertake programs to improve it. Maybe the National Federation of Priests' Councils will even fund a study by Dean Hoge of preaching and preparation of homilies—including a study of the reactions of parishioners.

Individual priests should consider mailing the NORC questionnaire on ministerial service (see chapter 6) to their parish list. They might establish parish oversight committees to challenge priests on the quality of their service, not unlike the national oversight committee headed by Justice Anne Burke to make sure the sexual abuse rules are enforced. They might also think about reading a little more, too. It's hard to write a decent sermon when you have not had a new idea in ten years.

Is it possible to do research on the qualities that make for good preaching and good ministerial service? It is possible but complicated and expensive. Nonetheless, one can-

1. This is not a joke. Most seminary training in homiletics is a joke. Some priests say to me, "You have writing talent, I don't. It's not fair that you demand that talent from me." In fact, while raw writing talent varies enormously from person to person, no one is genetically programmed to write. Everyone must work to learn how to do it. Unless one is willing to work so that one can write a decent sermon, one does not have a vocation to be a priest. Moreover, it is an insult to the laity, many of whom have to learn to talk on their feet, for a priest to bring his sermon to the pulpit and read it. An outline, maybe for the first couple of years, but no longer. If he needs psychotherapy or public-speaking training to preach well, then so be it. Let him get the training before ordination.

not escape the harsh fact that, as a ministerial profession, the priesthood has very serious problems. They are not new. They did not develop yesterday or last year or even with the Second Vatican Council (which gets blamed for everything these days). They will not go away tomorrow or the next day. However, the laity, who pay the bills, have a right to high-quality priestly service, in strict commutative justice with the obligation to restitution. Somehow priests must come to see that there is no substitute for excellence.

At every step in the training and the ongoing education of the clergy, in every planning committee, and at every meeting, retreat, prayer day for priests, the laity should be present, not to fight, not to demand, not to seize power, but to communicate, respectfully but honestly. The clergy as a collectivity and priests as individuals may pretend that the problems are not there, but the ocean is washing over the beaches in whose sands they have buried their heads. Clerical culture and its blind loyalty to the guys is in the final analysis the cause of the abuse scandal, not homosexuality or celibacy.

Finally, priests must assume responsibility for responding to the anger of the laity because of the sexual abuse scandal. It is not permissible for them to wash their hands of it. They must not content themselves with blaming bishops, the media, and the laity for the decline in church attendance and contributions. Much of the anger is also the result of their inadequate professional service, their cruelty in denying the sacraments, and their insensitivity to parishioners, especially, as they see it, to women parishioners.

It would be useful (and perhaps necessary) for priests' groups to take out ads in the papers saying in effect, "You think you're angry? We're angry too and angry at ourselves because we weren't alert enough to stop the abuse. You can count on us. We're not going to let it happen any more. And we're going to improve our preaching and our liturgy and make our rectories user friendly."

Such a declaration would begin to weaken the walls of clerical culture that stand behind the rectory door.

## BISHOPS AND THE YEAR
## OF THE PEDOPHILE

Even as the Year of the Pedophile came to an end, one heard stories of bishops that still don't get it. In some dioceses eager-beaver bishops on the make shamelessly violated the due process rights of priests. In other dioceses bishops still contended that the Dallas norms are to be enforced at the discretion of the bishop—which means that the bishop can play the same old game he has always played. The lay oversight board enacted at Dallas, men and women, it would seem, of great ability and forcefulness, have their work cut out for them.

Other bishops (especially some young auxiliaries on the make) have urged that there be a plenary council, a national meeting of bishops to legislate on matters of importance for the whole Church. While others would be able to attend the council, they would be named by the bishops, and the bishops would dominate it. The proposals for such a meeting (which would turn into yet another media circus) are that it concentrate on the authority of the bishop and on sound Catholic doctrine—the latter of which means sexual teaching. Such an assembly, those who propose it claim, would restore confidence in the leadership of the Church and create a sense of equanimity among the faithful.

One wonders how those who support such a scheme can possibly be so insensitive. A group of men whose behavior has stirred up the outrage of the Catholic laity propose to

gather together, legislate for the laity on sex, and by so doing restore their credibility. One imagines a meeting of the
Congress of the Confederate States of America in 1870 to
legislate again for the southern states on the restoration of
slavery. Before they try any further quests for power, bishops have to satisfy the laity that they have learned the lessons of the Year of the Pedophile and merit their confidence. That will be a long and difficult process because of
the deep and abiding anger of the laity. The bishops who
call for a restoration of trust (which means the laity must
trust them again) are still caught up in the clerical culture's
denial. Despite convincing evidence of decline in church
attendance and financial contributions, they think that it
is still business as usual in American Catholicism, that they
can still make demands and the laity will respond. They
have yet to understand the lessons of the Year of the Pedophile, chief of which is that bishops must be open, sensitive, and responsive to their laity. If they still don't comprehend this truth, it is unlikely they ever will.

The best policy strategy for bishops in these times con-
sists of humility, silence, caution, and a determination to
listen and learn. They should acknowledge that they made
a terrible mistake in covering up sexual abuse by priests
and then reassigning the abusers. They must admit to
themselves that these mistakes have stirred up a firestorm
of lay fury. They should try to understand the nature of
that fury through focus groups and high-quality annual surveys of their people. They must admit to themselves that
they don't know what's going on among the laity and that
they need to learn. Many American bishops, it is to be
feared, are constitutionally incapable of such humility.

They must also lead their priests in efforts to take off
the blinders of clerical culture and to improve the quality

of their ministerial service, especially in homilies and liturgy and kindness to the laity at the door and on the phone
line (in both parish and chancery office). They should try
to say yes whenever they can, instead of no whenever they
think they can get away with it. Such efforts, an absolutely
essential precondition for the restoration of confidence,
will require both hard work and persistence.

There are some American bishops who, like the auxiliary
quoted in the epigraph of this book, realize that they are in
an epochal crisis, the worst in the history of the American
church. Moreover, they also realize that this crisis is now
an essential part of the transition after the Second Vatican
Council. These men display a powerful sense of urgency
and a realization that the Church is continuing to implode.
The rules have changed. The same games can't be played
any more. Arrogance doesn't work. Authentic humility is
the only possible mode of response.

Many other bishops are clueless. They see no need to
change their styles. They continue to act like men who have
all the answers when they don't even know the questions.
They do not realize how foolish they seem and how much
they embarrass their laity when they appear on TV and ex-
ude the same old self-satisfied, triumphalist complacency.

Moreover their media relations apparatus, both local
and national, is unspeakably bad. If the media got most of
the sexual abuse story wrong, the reason in substantial part
is that most official spokespersons and media directors inside the hierarchy are obstructionist and obscurantist ca-
reerists. They appear more interested in the protection of
bishops from contact with journalists than in the facilita-
tion of the journalists' work and in the admonishment of
bishops when they make fools of themselves. Inability to
hire competent, honest professionals to intervene between

them and the media is a luxury bishops can no longer afford. It may be satisfying, but it is not helpful, to blame the media for the Church's problems.

Bishops may not want competent media advisers (preferably women and Jewish) around them, but it's high time they begin to understand that they must have them. Everyone in the business of communicating with the public—and bishops are certainly in that business—needs to pay someone to tell them when they have made a fool of themselves and that they should never again say something as dumb as they've just said. A man who is unwilling to take the risk of hearing that every day should resign and go to a monastery to spend his life in prayer and pious works.

## POLICY CHANGES FOR THE HOLY SEE

The leadership in the Vatican should realize that its easy, one-sentence analyses of the Church in the United States are self-deceptive and self-destructive. There are close to seventy-five million Catholics in this country, most of them loyal and dedicated Catholics. Most have lost their confidence in church leadership. If this confidence is to be restored, the process must begin now. It must involve the appointment of bishops who are in touch with their priests and laypeople, who know what's happening, and who can inspire confidence in the faithful.

Unfortunately the Vatican does not choose bishops for these qualities, though in some cases, I suspect more or less by accident, intelligent, able, and perceptive men do wear the sacred purple. More often, however, episcopal appointments are the result of a mix of cronyism and silent incompetence disguised as virtue.[2] The Church entered the Year

2. Many bishops will whisper that it is dangerous to speak out at a meeting because the spies among your colleagues will report you to Rome.

of the Pedophile with the average ability of the bench of bishops at perhaps an all-time low. The appointments during the year did not seem to reflect an awareness of what was happening. Either in years to come the Vatican will give up its proclivity to appoint men who are docile and diffident and make no waves, or the Church in the United States may eventually go the way the Church in Holland did.

The Vatican is for the most part made up of priests. Hence it is as subject to the infections of the same denial virus as every other level of clergy. The lower clergy describe their people in clichés, bishops respond to their clergy with clichés of their own, the Vatican appoints bishops according to guidelines that are thick with clichés. The lines of communication within the Church are stuffed with clichés. At no level does anyone listen. No one has any idea what's actually happening. Hence phenomena like the Year of the Pedophile.

In the short run I anticipate a reaction to 2002 like that to the birth-control encyclical—a decline in church attendance and a decline in financial contributions but no mass exodus from Catholicism. Catholics, even very angry Catholics, still like being Catholic.

This prognosis is a best-case scenario. In the worst case, the Catholic Church in the United States may suffer the fate of St. Augustine's diocese of Hippo in North Africa. It may go down the drain, but not because of attacking infidels, not because of celibacy or homosexuality or sexual abuse, not because of secularism and materialism, but because of incompetence, stupidity, and clerical culture—all enemies from within.

The cure? Clergy at all levels from the pope down to the lowliest parish curate must be quiet and listen. And listen. And listen.

# APPENDIX
## FROM THE *LOS ANGELES TIMES**

HOW THE POLL WAS CONDUCTED

### Overview

This survey is the 471st in a series of *Los Angeles Times* opinion studies designed to measure public attitudes on a number of critical issues. It is the second *Los Angeles Times* survey of Roman Catholic priests in the United States. The study takes a look at the attitudes of priests in the Roman Catholic Church in America today, in a period when the Church is undergoing public and private scrutiny. Although Catholic-affiliated surveys of the attitudes of priests have been done recently, no independent survey of this population has been taken since the Times Poll surveyed priests and nuns over a period of months in 1993 and 1994 (LAT surveys 321 and 323).

For this survey, 1,854 active and retired priests in 80 dioceses across the U.S. and in Puerto Rico returned mail-ballot questionnaires over the period June 27–Oct. 11. Diocesan and religious priests were included in the sample. Spanish language questionnaires were provided for priests in Puerto Rico.

### Sample Design and Coverage

The Times Poll selected 5,000 priests from a total population of 45,382 in the United States and Puerto Rico using a two-stage procedure.

First, the *Official Catholic Directory* (OFCD), published by P. J. Kennedy & Sons, was used to compile a complete list of all the dioceses in the country as well as the total priest population in each diocese. The list was pre-stratified by regional geography.

Eighty dioceses were randomly selected, proportional to priest population in each region.

For the second-stage sample selection, Times Poll researchers obtained directories for each of the sample dioceses wherever possible.

When such directories were either unavailable or actively withheld, the OFCD was substituted as a source. In this way, a sample of 5,000 active and retired priests was drawn in proportion to priest population in each diocesan area.

At this point, two Tribune newspapers—the *Morning Call* in Allentown, Pa., and the *South Florida Sun-Sentinel* in Ft. Lauderdale, Fl.—expressed an interest in over-sampling dioceses in their areas for national comparison. In order to provide enough data for separate analysis of the three southern Pa. dioceses of interest to the *Morning Call* (Scranton, Allentown and Philadelphia, of which only Scranton and Philadelphia were in the first-stage sample pick) and the two dioceses of interest to the *South Florida Sun-Sentinel* (Miami and Palm Beach, neither of which was in the original first-stage sample pick), every priest in those five dioceses was contacted.

Note that the data set under analysis here includes only the Times Poll's original selected priests in the Scranton and Philadelphia dioceses.[1]

---

1. Only the dioceses originally selected in the first stage and priests originally selected in the second stage of the sampling process are included in this data set. No interviews conducted in the dioceses of Allentown, Miami or Palm Beach have been included and the interviews with non-sampled priests are excluded as well.

The survey questionnaires were first mailed on June 27. This was after the Bishops' conference. Seven thousand two hundred and twenty-two questionnaires, cover letters and pre-paid return envelopes were sent. A second mailing of the same packet was sent to 5,878 non-responding priests on July 25. A reminder postcard was mailed to 5,707 non-responding priests on Aug. 5, and a final third set of 4,924 questionnaire packets was mailed to continuing non-responders on Sept. 4.[2] The end date of the survey was Oct. 11, making it a 16-week field period. In creating its design, the Times Poll followed the general guidelines for mail surveys found in Dillman's *Mail and Internet Surveys*.[3]

Research and field work for the 78 dioceses outside southern Pa. were completed by *Los Angeles Times* field staff[4] under the supervision of Times Poll Field Director Roger Richardson and Times Poll Director Susan Pinkus. Data collection in the dioceses of Philadelphia and Scranton, Pa., was overseen for the *Morning Call* newspaper by Chris Borick, assistant professor of political science at Muhlenberg College.

### Return Rates and Margins of Error

By the standard calculation for true random sample of a population of this size, one can say with 95% certainty that the margin of error for this sample is ±3 percentage points. All population surveys, including this one, are subject to errors of many kinds. Bias may be introduced through cov-

---

2. Fifty-five percent of the total completed and refused questionnaires had been returned by the date of the second mailing, 68% by the date of the reminder postcard mailing, and 88% by the date of the third and final mailing.

3. *Mail and Internet Surveys, The Tailored Design Method*, by Dillman, Don A., John Wiley & Sons, 2000 (2nd ed.).

4. The Times Poll would like to acknowledge supervisor Art Dodd and editors Walter Boxer, Debra Birgen and Cynthia Kirk for their diligence and hard work on this survey.

erage errors, survey non-response, question-wording issues and other types of human error. Every attempt was made to reduce all of these through preliminary research and follow-ups on non-responders. Four attempts were made to convince priests to return their questionnaires.

Using a response-rate calculation that removes deceased, unqualified and reassigned priests from the sample, resulting in a total sample size of 4,965, the survey has a type A response rate of 37%. Additional removal of unavailable priests results in a sample size of 4,887 and a type B response rate of 38%. Type A response rates ranged from 30% among dioceses in the South to 44% in the Midwest.

Response rate on this survey may have been affected by a variety of issues. First, the Roman Catholic priest population has been subject to intense media scrutiny over the last few months. Many non-responding priests indicated that their refusal to cooperate was due to a concern that their answers would be sensationalized by the press. There were various negative publications about this survey in the Catholic community. Despite the negative publicity, response rates were acceptable in all dioceses and outstanding in some.

In addition to response rate issues, undetected flaws in the way the sampling and interviewing procedure were carried out could have a significant effect on findings. Changing the wording of questions and the sequence in which they are asked can produce different results. Sometimes questions are inadvertently biased or misleading and people who respond to surveys may not necessarily replicate the views of those who refuse to participate. Moreover, while every precaution has been taken to make these findings completely accurate, other errors may have resulted from the various practical difficulties associated with taking any survey of public opinion.

Some of the best data available for comparison on this survey are surveys of priest populations conducted by Georgetown University's Center for Applied Research in the Apostolate (CARA). Comparing numbers of active and retired priests nationwide[5] to those in our survey, one can see that this survey slightly over-represents active diocesan priests and underrepresents religious priests.

| All US[5] | | LA Times Priests Poll 2002 |
|---|---|---|
| Diocesan, Active | 48 % | 54 % |
| Diocesan, Retired | 15 % | 14 % |
| Religious, Active | 31 % | 28 % |
| Religious, Retired | 6 % | 4 % |

Comparing sample population to the figures taken from the *Official Catholic Directory*, the sample slightly under-represents priests in the East and Midwest and over-represents those in the South. The sample figures have been adjusted slightly to account for this difference.

| All US Priests* | | LA Times Priests Poll 2002 |
|---|---|---|
| East | 38 % | 36 % |
| Midwest | 17 % | 13 % |
| South | 30 % | 35 % |
| West | 15 % | 16 % |

\* Figures calculated from population totals in *Official Catholic Directory* 2001.

The Los Angeles Times Poll is directed by Susan Pinkus under the general supervision of Los Angeles Times Managing Editor Dean Baquet. Jill Darling Richardson is the associate director, Roger Richardson is the field director, Clau-

---

5. National study of priests conducted by CARA in 1999 for the Committee for Priestly Life and Ministry of the United States Conference of Catholic Bishops.

dia Vaughn is the data management supervisor and Ray Enslow is the publications coordinator.

Further information regarding this study is available by writing to the Los Angeles Times Poll, 202 West 1st Street, Los Angeles, California 90012-4105, by calling (213) 237-2027 or by e-mailing *timespoll@latimes.com*. Times Poll data is also available online at *www.latimes.com/timespoll*.

This report conforms to the standards of disclosure of the National Council on Public Polls and the American Association for Public Opinion Research.

# The Los Angeles Times Poll

SURVEY OF ROMAN CATHOLIC PRIESTS

**Los Angeles Times**

*This is a confidential survey. Please do not sign your name.*

For each question, please check the box next to your answer; if a question calls for a response in your own words, write it on the lines provided beneath the question. There is additional space on the last page of the questionnaire for your general comments or suggestions. Thank you for your cooperation.

---

**1. Your age is:**

_____ years

**2. The last grade of education you completed is:**

1. ☐ High school graduate or less
2. ☐ Two-year college
3. ☐ Four-year college
4. ☐ Master's degree
5. ☐ Doctoral degree
6. ☐ Post-graduate work

**3. How many years have you been a priest, that is, counting back to when you were ordained?**
*(if less than one year, write "1")*

_____ years

**4. Are you a diocesan priest or are you a member of an order?** *(if belong to order)* **To which order do you belong?**

001. ☐ Diocesan priest
002. ☐ Member of order:
         *(write in full name of order)* _____

_____

**5. Which of the following best describes your principal assignment as a priest?**

01. ☐ Retired, semi-retired
02. ☐ Pastor of a parish
03. ☐ Curate, assistant pastor
04. ☐ Some other parish assignment
05. ☐ Administration
06. ☐ Education, teaching
07. ☐ Chaplain
08. ☐ Itinerant preacher
09. ☐ Other: *(write in answer)* _____

_____

**6. Are you an external priest in this diocese, or not?**

1. ☐ Yes          2. ☐ No

**7. Were you raised in the United States or in some other country?**

01. ☐ United States
02. ☐ Other country: *(write in country name)* _____

_____

**8. If you were raised in another country, how long have you been living in the United States?**
*(if less than one year, write "1")*

_____ years

**9. Are you of Latino or Hispanic descent—for example, Mexican, or Puerto Rican, or Cuban, or some other Spanish background?**

1. ☐ Yes, Latino          2. ☐ No, not Latino

**10. Is your race:**

1. ☐ White          3. ☐ Asian or Pacific Islander
2. ☐ Black          4. ☐ Something else

**11. What are the greatest joys that you receive in your life and work as a priest today?**

_____
_____
_____
_____
_____
_____
_____
_____
_____

12. What are the greatest challenges you face in your
    life and work as a priest today?

_____

_____

_____

_____

_____

_____

_____

_____

_____

13. All things considered, would you say you are satis-
    fied or dissatisfied with the way your life as a priest is
    going these days?

    1. ☐ Very satisfied
    2. ☐ Somewhat satisfied
    3. ☐ Somewhat dissatisfied
    4. ☐ Very dissatisfied

14. Has your life as a priest turned out:

    1. ☐ Better than you expected
    2. ☐ Worse than you expected
    3. ☐ About as you expected

15. If you had the opportunity to make the choice over
    again, would you:

    1. ☐ Definitely enter the priesthood
    2. ☐ Probably enter the priesthood
    3. ☐ Probably not enter the priesthood
    4. ☐ Definitely not enter the priesthood

16. If a promising young man came to you today for
    advice as to whether he should enter the seminary
    and become a priest, would you advise that young
    man to enter the priesthood today or not?

    1. ☐ Yes, would recommend
    2. ☐ No, would not recommend

17. If you would not recommend that he enter the sem-
    inary, why not?

_____

_____

_____

_____

_____

18. What are the chances that, in the next few years,
    you might leave the priesthood?

    1. ☐ Very likely          3. ☐ Somewhat unlikely
    2. ☐ Somewhat likely      4. ☐ Very unlikely

## Now turning your attention to the papacy of Pope John Paul II...

19. How do you think Pope John Paul II will be
    remembered by history?

    1. ☐ As an outstanding pope
    2. ☐ As an above-average pope
    3. ☐ As an average pope
    4. ☐ As a below-average pope
    5. ☐ As a poor pope

20. In your opinion, are Pope John Paul II's views on
    moral issues generally:

    1. ☐ Too liberal
    2. ☐ Too conservative
    3. ☐ About right

21. Thinking now about Pope John Paul II's papacy,
    what accomplishments do you think he will be best
    remembered for?

_____

_____

_____

_____

_____

_____

_____

_____

2

22. As you know, many of Pope John Paul II's accomplishments are admired by Catholics and non-Catholics around the world. Thinking now about the election of the next pope, are there any issues or characteristics commonly associated with Pope John Paul II's papacy that you would like the next pope to continue?

_____

_____

_____

_____

_____

_____

_____

23. Again, thinking about the election of the next pope, are there any issues or characteristics not commonly associated with Pope John Paul II's papacy that you hope the next pope will pursue? What are they?

_____

_____

_____

_____

_____

_____

Thinking now about issues in your diocese...

24. Overall, do you approve or disapprove of the way the bishop who presides in your diocese is handling his duties?

1. ☐ Approve strongly    3. ☐ Disapprove somewhat
2. ☐ Approve somewhat    4. ☐ Disapprove strongly

25. In your opinion, are the views of the bishop of your diocese on moral issues generally:

1. ☐ Too liberal       3. ☐ About right
2. ☐ Too conservative

26. When you need counsel and guidance, how comfortable do you feel about going to your bishop or to the superiors of your order?

1. ☐ Very comfortable     3. ☐ Fairly uncomfortable
2. ☐ Fairly comfortable   4. ☐ Very uncomfortable

27. Would you favor or oppose direct democratic election of diocesan bishops by the diocesan clergy and laity in the U.S.?

1. ☐ Favor strongly    3. ☐ Oppose somewhat
2. ☐ Favor somewhat    4. ☐ Oppose strongly

Thinking now about the Catholic Church in the United States...

28. What are the most important problems facing the Roman Catholic Church in the United States today?

_____

_____

_____

_____

_____

29. Overall, would you rate things in the Catholic Church in America today as:

1. ☐ Excellent    3. ☐ Not so good
2. ☐ Good         4. ☐ Poor

30. Would you say things in the Catholic Church in America are generally:

1. ☐ Getting better
2. ☐ Getting worse
3. ☐ Staying about the same

31. How much confidence do you have in the Catholic Church in America today?

1. ☐ A great deal    3. ☐ Not much
2. ☐ Some            4. ☐ None at all

32. Generally speaking, do you think younger priests in America are more theologically conservative—that is, more religiously orthodox—than their older counterparts, or are they more liberal, or are they just about the same?

1. ☐ Much more conservative
2. ☐ Somewhat more conservative
3. ☐ About the same
4. ☐ Somewhat more liberal
5. ☐ Much more liberal

33. Generally speaking, would you say that younger priests today are more theologically conservative than they were in the 1970s and 1980s, or are they more liberal, or have priests stayed about the same theologically?

1. ☐ Much more conservative
2. ☐ Somewhat more conservative
3. ☐ About the same
4. ☐ Somewhat more liberal
5. ☐ Much more liberal

34. Do you think the Catholic Church needs to be reformed in any way, or not? If you think the Church needs to be reformed, what kind of reform do you think is needed in the Catholic Church?

01. ☐ Reform is not needed
02. ☐ The following reform is needed:
*(write in answer)*_____

_____

_____

_____

_____

_____

_____

35. If you think the Church needs to be reformed, do you think reform should proceed quickly in the Church or should it proceed slowly?

1. ☐ Should proceed quickly
2. ☐ Should proceed slowly

36. Do you think Roman Catholics must follow all of the Church's teachings to be faithful, or do you think they may disagree on some issues and still be considered faithful?

1. ☐ Must follow all teachings
2. ☐ May disagree and be faithful

37. To what degree do you agree or disagree with the statement: "The sole path to salvation is through faith in Jesus Christ"?

1. ☐ Agree strongly     3. ☐ Disagree somewhat
2. ☐ Agree somewhat     4. ☐ Disagree strongly

## Now turning to the Catholic laity...

38. What are the greatest problems that the laity you come into contact with face as practicing Catholics?

01. ☐ I don't come into contact with the laity
02. ☐ The greatest problems are: *(write in answer)*

_____

_____

_____

_____

_____

39. Do you think families in this country today are threatened more by: *(check only one answer)*

01. ☐ An economic climate that makes finding jobs and affordable health care difficult
02. ☐ A moral climate that hurts community standards and strong family units
03. ☐ Both equally
04. ☐ Something else: *(write in answer)*_____

_____

_____

40. Are the laity you come in contact with these days most in need of: *(check only one answer)*

1. ☐ Spiritual guidance and fulfillment
2. ☐ Guidance on moral issues
3. ☐ Help with temporal (family, job and economic) issues
4. ☐ I don't come into contact with the laity

41. When it comes to moral issues, such as sexuality, marriage and reproduction, are most of the Catholic laity you come in contact with:

1. ☐ Following the Church's teachings
2. ☐ Going their own way
3. ☐ I don't come into contact with the laity

42. In your opinion, what are the principal reasons laity are leaving the Church these days?

_____

_____

_____

_____

_____

_____

_____

43. Do you think it is always, often, seldom or never a sin: (check one box on each line)

|  | Always 1. | Often 2. | Seldom 3. | Never 4. |
|---|---|---|---|---|
| A) ...for unmarried people to have sexual relations? | ☐ | ☐ | ☐ | ☐ |
| B) ...for a woman to get an abortion? | ☐ | ☐ | ☐ | ☐ |
| C) ...for married couples to use artificial methods of birth control? | ☐ | ☐ | ☐ | ☐ |
| D) ...to use cloning—that is, copying DNA cells—in medical research that could result in a cure for diseases such as Alzheimer's, Parkinson's or cancer? | ☐ | ☐ | ☐ | ☐ |
| E) ...to use stem cells of fetuses for medical research? | ☐ | ☐ | ☐ | ☐ |
| F) ...to use condoms as a protection against AIDS? | ☐ | ☐ | ☐ | ☐ |
| G) ...to engage in homosexual behavior? | ☐ | ☐ | ☐ | ☐ |
| H) ...to take one's own life if one is suffering from a debilitating disease? | ☐ | ☐ | ☐ | ☐ |
| I) ...to masturbate? | ☐ | ☐ | ☐ | ☐ |

## Turning now to some other issues in the Catholic Church in America...

44. Would you favor or oppose:
*(check one box on each line)*

|  | — Favor — | | —Oppose— | |
|---|---|---|---|---|
|  | strongly 1. | somewhat 2. | somewhat 3. | strongly 4. |
| A) ...the ordination of women as deacons? | ☐ | ☐ | ☐ | ☐ |
| B) ...the ordination of women as priests? | ☐ | ☐ | ☐ | ☐ |
| C) ...the ordination of women as bishops? | ☐ | ☐ | ☐ | ☐ |

45. Regardless of whether you favor or oppose it, which of the following statements do you think is the most compelling reason for ordaining women as priests? *(check only one answer)*

1. ☐ It would increase the number of priests/reduce the shortage
2. ☐ Women's equality is important to American society and the Church should reflect the society it serves
3. ☐ Women could provide an important voice in the Church's response to sexual abuse allegations
4. ☐ Women in the priesthood would reduce the instances of sexual abuse
5. ☐ Women's spiritual gifts would enhance the life and ministry of the Church

46. Would you favor or oppose the ordination of married priests in the Latin Rite?

1. ☐ Favor strongly
2. ☐ Favor somewhat
3. ☐ Oppose somewhat
4. ☐ Oppose strongly

47. Regardless of whether you favor or oppose the ordination of married priests in the Latin Rite, which of the following statements do you think is the most compelling reason for allowing the ordination of married priests? *(check only one answer)*

1. ☐ To help reduce the shortage of priests
2. ☐ It would make the priesthood more representative of the laity
3. ☐ It would help priests understand married and family life better
4. ☐ It would reduce instances of sexual abuse of minors

48. Do you think the Church will ever again allow the ordination of married priests in the Latin Rite or do you think that will never happen? *(if yes)* When do you think that will happen?

1. ☐ Married priests will never again be ordained
2. ☐ In less than 20 years
3. ☐ In 20 years or more

49. In your opinion, has the shortage of priests caused the Church to lower its standards in admitting men to the seminaries, or are standards higher, or are standards about where they have always been?

1. ☐ Lower
2. ☐ Higher
3. ☐ Same

50. Do you think the U.S. news media's treatment of the Catholic Church is:

1. ☐ Positive
2. ☐ Fair
3. ☐ Negative

51. Would you describe your views on most matters having to do with religious beliefs and moral doctrines as:

1. ☐ Very liberal       4. ☐ Somewhat conservative
2. ☐ Somewhat liberal   5. ☐ Very conservative
3. ☐ Middle-of-the-road

52. Would you describe your views on most matters having to do with politics as:

1. ☐ Very liberal       4. ☐ Somewhat conservative
2. ☐ Somewhat liberal   5. ☐ Very conservative
3. ☐ Middle-of-the-road

Some people have suggested that there are homosexual subcultures in some seminaries, dioceses and religious institutes. A "subculture" refers to a definite group of persons that has its own friendships, social gatherings and vocabulary.

53. Would you say there is a homosexual subculture in your diocese or religious institute, or not? How certain are you?

1. ☐ Yes, definitely
2. ☐ I think so but I'm not positive
3. ☐ I don't think so
4. ☐ No, definitely not

54. Thinking now about the seminary or seminaries you attended, was there a homosexual subculture there at the time, or not? How certain are you?

1. ☐ Yes, definitely
2. ☐ I think so but I'm not positive
3. ☐ I don't think so
4. ☐ No, definitely not

55. Some people think of themselves as heterosexual in orientation, while others think of themselves as homosexual in orientation and still others feel their sexual orientation lies somewhere in between. How about you?

1. ☐ Heterosexual orientation
2. ☐ Somewhere in between, but more on the heterosexual side
3. ☐ Completely in the middle
4. ☐ Somewhere in between, but more on the homosexual side
5. ☐ Homosexual orientation

56. Which of the following statements most closely describes how you feel about the role that celibacy plays in your life?

1. ☐ Celibacy is not a problem for me and I do not waver in my vows
2. ☐ Celibacy takes time to achieve and I consider it an ongoing journey
3. ☐ Celibacy is a discipline I try to follow, but do not always succeed
4. ☐ Celibacy is not relevant to my priesthood and I do not observe it

57. Generally speaking, would you say celibacy is easier for priests with a heterosexual orientation, or is celibacy easier for priests who have a homosexual orientation, or would you say it is the same regardless of orientation?

1. ☐ Easier for heterosexuals
2. ☐ Easier for homosexuals
3. ☐ Same regardless of orientation

58. As you know, intimacy may be defined as a basic human need that includes close non-sexual bonds with personal friends. How satisfied are you with the level of that type of intimacy in your life?

1. ☐ I am very satisfied
2. ☐ I am mostly satisfied
3. ☐ I am neither satisfied nor dissatisfied
4. ☐ I am mostly dissatisfied
5. ☐ I am very dissatisfied

The next few questions are about the current allegations of child sexual abuse by priests. Please remember that this is a confidential, anonymous survey. Your answers will be published only as a percentage of those answering.

*If you are not comfortable in answering any one question, please skip it and move on to the next one. However, each of your answers is extremely valuable for the success of the survey and we hope you will want your opinions to be fully represented. Thank you.*

59. Generally speaking, do you approve or disapprove of the way bishops have handled allegations of child sexual abuse against their diocesan priests?

1. ☐ Approve strongly      3. ☐ Disapprove somewhat
2. ☐ Approve somewhat    4. ☐ Disapprove strongly

60. Thinking now about the recent allegations of sexual misconduct by priests… Do you think that most, many, some or only a few of the allegations are true?

1. ☐ Most          3. ☐ Some
2. ☐ Many          4. ☐ Only a few

61. When it comes to disciplining priests accused of child sexual abuse, would you say the Church has:

1. ☐ Been too harsh      3. ☐ Done just about the
2. ☐ Been too lenient          right thing

62. Thinking about the compact approved by the Bishops' Conference in June… Overall, how satisfied are you that the bishops' compact adequately addresses the issues dealing with child sexual abuse by priests?

1. ☐ Completely satisfied
2. ☐ Mostly satisfied
3. ☐ Somewhat satisfied
4. ☐ Neither satisfied nor dissatisfied
5. ☐ Somewhat dissatisfied
6. ☐ Mostly dissatisfied
7. ☐ Completely dissatisfied

63. Please rate how well the bishops' compact addresses the following issues: *(check one box on each line)*

|  | Excellent 1. | Good 2. | Neutral 3. | Fair 4. | Poor 5. |
|---|---|---|---|---|---|
| A) Restoring confidence in the Catholic Church | ☐ | ☐ | ☐ | ☐ | ☐ |
| B) Protecting minors from sexual abuse by priests | ☐ | ☐ | ☐ | ☐ | ☐ |
| C) Being fair to priests who are accused of abuse | ☐ | ☐ | ☐ | ☐ | ☐ |
| D) Providing for discipline of bishops who cover up for abusive priests | ☐ | ☐ | ☐ | ☐ | ☐ |

64. In your diocese, had an adequate procedure or mechanism been established *before* the Bishops' Conference for dealing with the issue of child sexual abuse by priests?

1. ☐ Yes          2. ☐ No

65. Do you agree or disagree with the following statement: "The Catholic Church in America is now facing its biggest crisis in the last century"?

1. ☐ Strongly agree       3. ☐ Disagree, not strongly
2. ☐ Agree, not strongly  4. ☐ Strongly disagree

66. Thinking about the recent allegations, what one aspect of the crisis bothers you the most, or aren't you bothered by anything in particular?

01. ☐ Nothing in particular
02. ☐ What bothers me the most:
       *(write in answer)*_____

_____

_____

_____

_____

67. As you are aware, the Bishops' Conference did not address the issue of disciplining bishops. If a bishop is found to have protected a priest who has sexually abused a minor, what do you think should happen to the bishop? Should he:

1. ☐ Not apologize, impose new safeguards and continue to serve
2. ☐ Apologize, impose new safeguards and continue to serve
3. ☐ Apologize, impose new safeguards and resign his post
4. ☐ Be arrested for aiding and abetting a criminal

*You may have comments about our questions. Please feel free to write them in the space on the following page.*

---

*Thank you for your participation.*

This questionnaire is anonymous.
*Do not sign your name.*

If you wish to contact us to ask questions about the survey or to talk to a reporter, you may call us toll-free at

1·800·LATPOLL Extension 70005

7

What have we left out that you would like to talk about?
Please use the space below for your comments, suggestions or concerns.

*Thank you for your participation.*
This questionnaire is anonymous. Do not sign your name.

Survey of Roman Catholic Priests

**Los Angeles Times**

202 West First Street
Los Angeles, CA 90012
213 237 7993

June 26, 2002

**Susan H. Pinkus**
Times Poll Director

Dear Reverend Father:

The Los Angeles Times is conducting its second extensive nationwide survey of Catholic priests in America, with the goal of better understanding the issues and challenges facing the church today. There have been many national polls recently analyzing how Catholics and the public in general feel about the issues affecting the Catholic Church. But, it is also important to hear from the priests in their own voices and to gauge their attitudes on various issues affecting the church. The information you provide will help us contextualize issues in the church that have been oversimplified and perhaps not adequately presented to the public. Our goal is to better understand the realities facing priests today, the overwhelming majority of whom are serving faithfully.

Your name was picked at random from lists of priests in dozens of dioceses across the nation. Over the next week or ten days, we respectfully request that you take the time to fill out the enclosed confidential questionnaire and return it to us in the self-addressed envelope provided. As you may remember, the Times conducted a similar survey in 1994 and published the results in a series of articles. You can review the results of that survey on our web site: *http:/www.latimes.com/news/custom/timespoll/la-940220cathpoll.story.*

This survey is confidential and anonymous. Please do not sign your name. Answers from individual questionnaires will be merged with hundreds of others and reported as percentages in an effort to represent the feelings of priests nationwide. Your participation will ensure that your views are registered as part of the overall findings. We wish to assure you of our desire to represent your views accurately and without bias, whatever they may be.

The Los Angeles Times is one of the oldest daily newspapers in the United States. We founded our survey research operation in 1978, and since then we have conducted hundreds of polls of Americans and special publics such as lawyers, doctors, judges, police officers, and military personnel.

The results of our survey will be published in The Times later in the year. We will be happy to send you a copy of those stories and a full report on the poll results as soon as they are available. Should you wish a copy of the survey findings, please do not include your name when you mail back the questionnaire. Instead you may call us toll free at 1-800-LATPOLL (1-800-528-7655) between the hours of 10:00 a.m. and 6:00 p.m. Pacific Daylight Time. Please also feel free to use this number should you have any questions or comments about our survey.

We have provided space for you to record your verbatim comments at the end of the questionnaire. Your thoughts are of great interest to us and we may wish to quote them in our stories, again anonymously. If by chance you wish to speak to our religion writer, either confidentially or on the record, please call us at 1-800-LATPOLL and an interview will be arranged at your convenience.

Father, please accept my best wishes and my thanks for taking the time to cooperate with our survey effort.

Sincerely yours,

*Susan H. Pinkus*

# Los Angeles Times

202 West First Street
Los Angeles, CA 90012
213 237-7993

**Susan H. Pinkus**
Times Poll Director

July 25, 2002

Dear Reverend Father:

The Los Angeles Times is in the process of conducting its second extensive nationwide survey of Roman Catholic priests in America, with the goal of better understanding the issues and challenges facing the church in America today. The Times feels that it is important to hear from the priests in their own voices and to gauge their attitudes on various issues affecting the church. The information you provide will help us contextualize issues in the church that have been oversimplified and perhaps not adequately presented to the public. Our goal is to better understand the realities facing priests today, the overwhelming majority of whom are serving faithfully.

Your name was picked at random from lists of priests in dozens of dioceses across the country. A few weeks ago we mailed you a questionnaire. We are concerned that the survey may not have reached you, and it is very important to us that your opinions be recorded as part of our effort. Accordingly, we are providing you with another copy of the questionnaire, identical in content to the one previously sent. Over the next few days, we respectfully request that you take the time to fill it out and return it to us in the envelope provided.

If by chance you have already received and mailed a form back to us, please disregard this letter and feel free to discard this new survey. If you now have two copies of the survey, please fill out just one and return it to us in the envelope provided. The survey is confidential and anonymous, so please do not sign your name. We wish to assure you of our desire to represent your views accurately and without bias, whatever they may be.

In the next month, we will be publishing the results of our findings in articles in *The Los Angeles Times*. We will be happy to provide you with a copy of those stories as well as a full summary of the survey results. If you wish to have that material mailed to you, please do not include your name and address when you return your survey. Instead, you may call us toll free at 1-800-LATPOLL (1-800-528-7655) on weekdays between the hours of 10AM and 6PM Pacific Standard Time (which is 1PM-9PM Eastern Standard Time). You may also use this number to ask questions or make comments about the survey or to make an appointment to speak to the Times' religion writer.

Father, let me once again emphasize how important it is for us to have your views on church issues included as part of the survey. Please accept my best wishes and thanks for taking the time to participate with our survey effort.

Sincerely yours,

**August 5, 2002**

**Dear Reverend Father:**

Last week a questionnaire seeking your opinions about the issues and challenges facing the church in America today was mailed to you. Your name was chosen at random from lists of priests in dozens of dioceses across the country.

If you have already completed and returned the questionnaire to us, please accept our sincere thanks. If not, please do so today. We are especially grateful for your help because it is only by asking priests like yourself to share your experiences that we can better understand the realities facing priests today.

If you did not receive a questionnaire, or if it was misplaced, please call us at **1-800-LAT POLL (528-7655)** and we will get another one in the mail to you today. If you have any questions, please feel free to call us and use the same number.

*Susan H. Pinkus*

**Susan H. Pinkus**
Director, Los Angeles Times Poll

## Los Angeles Times

202 West First Street
Los Angeles, CA 90012
213 237-7993

September 4, 2002

**Susan H. Pinkus**
Times Poll Director

Dear Reverend Father:

About three weeks ago, we mailed a survey to a random selection of priests across the country to ask about their experiences in the priesthood. If you have already received one of these surveys and sent it back to us, we want to thank you very much for your participation. Please disregard this letter and feel free to discard this new survey. If you have not yet filled out the survey, we would like to make the case for your participation.

We are writing again because of the importance of your response to the accuracy of our survey. We have made every effort to write as clear and impartial a survey as possible, created in consultation with researchers and sociologists in the Catholic community. In choosing priests for this survey we adhered to strict methodological procedures which conformed to the guidelines set forth by the American Association for Public Opinion Research and the National Council on Public Polls.

As you may know, this is the second study of priests the Times Poll has undertaken. The first study was conducted in 1994. You may view the stories that were written and the results on that survey by visiting our web site at http://www.latimes.com/news/custom/timespoll/la-940220cathpoll.story, or you may call me directly and request that the stories be mailed directly to you. The Los Angeles Times religion writers are considered some of the best in the country and will, of course, treat the data gathered with the respect it deserves. All of the Times Poll's survey research data is published not only in the newspaper, but also online, and is archived at the Roper Center For Public Opinion Research at the University of Connecticut where any researcher who is interested may access the data directly.

We hope that you will choose to fill out and return the questionnaire, but if for any reason you prefer to abstain, please let us know by returning a note or blank questionnaire in the enclosed stamped envelope. The results of this survey will be published in the Times later in the year. We will be happy to send you a copy of those stories and a full report on the poll results as soon as they are available. If you would like a copy of the results or if you have any questions, please feel free to contact me at 1-800-LATPOLL.

Father, let me once again emphasize how important it is for your voices on church issues to be included as part of the study and to remind you that the answers are confidential and anonymous. Please accept my best wishes and thanks for taking the time to participate with our survey effort.

Sincerely yours,

*Susan H. Pinkus*

# REFERENCES

American Bar Association. 2001. *Career Satisfaction*. Young Lawyers Division.

Carroll, Jackson. 2002. "At Ease in Zion: Clergy Commitment and Satisfaction." Duke Divinity School.

Chaves, Mark. 1999. *Ordaining Women: Culture and Conflict in Religious Organizations*. Cambridge: Harvard University Press.

Cozzens, Donald B. 2000. *The Changing Face of the Priesthood: A Reflection on the Priest's Crisis of Soul*. Collegeville, Minnesota: Liturgical Press.

Greeley, Andrew. 1991. *Faithful Attraction: Discovering Intimacy, Love, and Fidelity in American Marriage*. New York: Tor Books.

———. 2003. *The Catholic Revolution: New Wine, Old Wineskins, and the Impact of Vatican II*. Berkeley: University of California Press.

Greeley, Andrew, and Mary G. Durkin. 1984. *Angry Catholic Women*. Chicago: Thomas More Press.

Greeley, Andrew, with William McCready, Teresa Sullivan, and Joan Fee. 1981. *Young Catholic Adults*. New York: Sadlier.

Hoge, Dean R. 2002. *The First Five Years: A Study of Newly Ordained Catholic Priests*. Collegeville, Minnesota: Liturgical Press.

Jones, L. Gregory. 2002. "Take This Job." *Christian Century*, August 14.

Kaiser Family Foundation. 2002. *National Survey of Physicians*.

Kennedy, Eugene C., and Victor Heckler. 1972. *The Catholic Priest in the United States: Psychological Investigations*. Washington, D.C.: United States Catholic Conference.

Kennedy, Eugene C. 2001. *The Unhealed Wound: The Church and Human Sexuality*. New York: St. Martin's.

Laumann, Edward O., John H. Gagnon, Robert T. Michael, and Stuart Michaels. 1994. *The Social Organization of Sexuality: Sexual Practices in the United States*. Chicago: University of Chicago Press.

Maslow, Abraham. 1962. *Towards a Psychology of Being*. New York: Van Nostrand.

McDonough, Peter, and Eugene Bianchi. 2001. *Passionate Uncertainty: Inside the American Jesuits*. Berkeley: University of California Press.

Michael, Robert. "Why Did the U.S. Divorce Rate Double within a Decade?" *Research in Population Economics* 6:367–99.

Money, John. 1968. *Sex Errors of the Body: Dilemmas, Education, Counseling*. Baltimore: Johns Hopkins University Press.

National Opinion Research Center (NORC). 1972. *The Catholic Priest in the United States: Sociological Investigations*. Washington, D.C.: United States Catholic Conference.

Nestor, Thomas. 1993. "Intimacy and Adjustment among Catholic Priests." Ph.D. dissertation, Loyola University, Chicago.

Sanderson, Allen. 2000. *The American Faculty Poll*. New York: TIAA-CREF.

Schoenherr, Richard. 1993. *Full Pews and Empty Altars: Demographics of the Priest Shortage in United States Catholic Dioceses*. Madison: University of Wisconsin Press.

————. 2002. *Goodbye Father: The Celibate Catholic Priesthood and the Future of the Catholic Church*. New York: Oxford University Press.

Sewell, William. 1996. "Three Temporalities: Toward an 'Eventful' Sociology." In *The Historical Turn in the Human Sciences*, edited by Terrence J. McDonald. Ann Arbor: University of Michigan Press.

Shostrom, E. L. 1963. *Personal Orientation Inventory*. San Diego: Educational and Industrial Testing Service.

Sipe, A. W. Richard. 1990. *A Secret World: Sexuality and the Search for Celibacy*. New York: Brunner/Mazel.

————. 1995. *Sex, Priests, and Power: Anatomy of a Crisis*. New York: Brunner/ Mazel.

Smith, Tom. 1999. "The Emerging 21st Century American Family." General Social Survey Social Change Report no. 42. Chicago: National Opinion Research Center (NORC).

Wilde, Melissa Jo. 2002. "Reconstructing Religion: A Sociological Study of Vatican Council II." Ph.D. dissertation, University of California, Berkeley.

# INDEX